Best Practices in
BUILDING YOUR PERSONAL NETWORK – for Attorneys

*BY: ALLAN BORESS, CPA, CFE
AND MICHAEL CUMMINGS*

Cover graphic courtesy of istockphoto
Print layout & design by somethingelse web+graphics

http://www.SAGElawmarketing.com
http://www.AllanBoress.com

ISBN: 0-9709337-3-8

Published by
SAGE Professional
37006 N. Thrill Hill Road
Eustis, FL 32736
PHONE (954) 345-4666   FAX (352) 483-5564
E-MAIL: info@sageprofessional.com

ALLAN S. BORESS, CPA, CFE

Allan S. Boress has been a Business Development Consultant to the professions since 1980.

Nobody we can find has trained more professionals in the arts of systematic selling, personal marketing, client retention, staff retention and motivation, and 21st Century Leadership—over 200,000 and worked with over 500 professional firms. He is acknowledged as the "Dean of Sales Consulting to the Professions."

An internationally-known speaker, trainer, and practice development expert, Mr. Boress was twice-named One of the **Top 100 People in the Accounting Profession** by *Accounting Today Magazine.* He is the author of eight published books, including *The I Hate Selling Book*: The only learning system ever custom-designed from scratch to teach professional service providers how to interview, qualify, present and close more sales opportunities. He is also the author of *Building Entrepreneurial People,* the only book that describes how to change the culture in a professional firm from business development reactivity to proactivity (available at Amazon.com). *The American Institute of CPAs* published his *Mastering the Art of Marketing Professional Services: A Step-by-step Best Practices Guide.*

Allan's training is the only one of its kind based upon the Best Practices of The Top Business Producers across the professions. Over 1,000 multi-million dollar rainmakers have been interviewed, studied and analyzed for this book, and for all of his writings and training programs. Mr. Boress is available for firm retreats, keynote speaking engagements, and on-site presentations. He is an award winning speaker and instructor. He is acknowledged as creator of the *"Professional's Selling System."* He may be contacted at www.allanboress.com or mailto:allan@allanboress.com

MICHAEL G. CUMMINGS

Mr. Cummings is the managing principal of SAGE. He has been a marketing strategy and business development consultant for over 20 years.

Early in his career, Michael was an instrumental member of the team that established the headquarters strategy and marketing function at Andersen Worldwide (Arthur Andersen & Accenture).

In this role, he defined information technology needs for key industries and functional areas; worked with senior partners to devise marketing plans and implement integrated marketing campaigns and developed strategy and marketing processes such as account management and market planning. He also helped to develop the initial large account management planning process and relationship management training programs.

Over the years, Michael has collaborated with Allan Boress to build the sales, marketing and relationship management skills of professionals. Based on their collective experience in working with the top business generators in the consulting, systems integration and accounting professions— they have translated proven best practices into practical, reality based skill building systems and training programs. And he co-authored a new book with Allan in 2002—*Mastering the Art of Marketing Professional Services: A Step-by-step Best Practices Guide (AICPA).*

Prior to establishing SAGE, Michael was partner at Mercer Management Consulting—a leading business design consulting firm. At Mercer, he was responsible for new business development, managing client relationships and delivering business design engagements in the communications, information and industrial industries.

In this role, he was a leader of Mercer's top North American account over the past 6 years: IBM. Using his account planning, relationship management and selling skills developed over the years, Michael helped Mercer to create over 300 senior executive relationships and sustained base of business. He also led account teams aimed at expanding relationships with Motorola, Siemens and NCR.

BIOGRAPHIES

CHAPTER 1

CHAPTER 2

CHAPTER 3

BUILDING YOUR PERSONAL NETWORK

CHAPTER 4

CHAPTER 5

HOW TO FOCUS ON YOUR BEST OPPORTUNITIES:
DEFINING YOUR PERSONAL MARKETING STRATEGY. 79

CHAPTER 6

THE ART OF MARKETING TO YOUR EXISTING CLIENTS. 103

CHAPTER 7

BUILDING POWERFUL MARKETING ALLIANCES. 123

PROVEN MARKETING PROGRAMS 134

CHAPTER 8

A SYSTEMATIC APPROACH THAT GUARANTEES QUALITY REFERRALS 145

CHAPTER 9

CHAPTER 10

CHAPTER 11

AFTERWORD

TOPIC INDEX

CHAPTER 1

INTRODUCTION BY ALLAN S. BORESS

NOTE:

Best Practices In Building Your Personal Network is drawn from our full scale program—*Best Practices In Legal Marketing*. The *Legal Marketing* program fully and more broadly explores personal marketing options beyond network building, options we occasionally refer to in this book and discuss briefly.

Still, as the present book demonstrates, we consider effective building of personal networks to be the lynchpin of all effective personal marketing. And this book is fully inclusive of all the network building best practices that you need to grow your practice. To underscore the necessity for taking action, we have included the introductory sections (Chapters 2 and 3) which lay out the case for more productive personal marketing in the legal profession.

THE PURPOSE OF THIS COURSE

New business is the life-blood of every law firm.

Some firms today are going out of business, being forced into mergers, surrendering superb talent, losing valued clients, being bought out or slowly disintegrating before everyone's eyes because not enough new clients and profitable new work are coming in to sustain the firm and pay off the partners who want to retire.

The purpose of this course, *Best Practices in Building Your Personal Network* is to share with you what I have learned over the last twenty-plus years as the top business development consultant to the professions. My goal is to provide you with a proven, methodical way to build your practice through your network building and make it more profitable and enjoyable for you.

In this course we will teach you how to avoid many of the "traps" of ineffective network building which can be extremely costly, time consuming and disheartening. You will find no theory in this course, only what produces the best possible results from the "personal marketing" effort.

Based on our 20 years of experience working with the top rainmakers in the legal profession, we are certain of one essential lesson you must learn to have a successful career as a practicing attorney.

Here it is. ***The top rainmakers see themselves as experts in the relationship business***. Simply put, the top producers have consciously and systematically built a ***comprehensive network of vital relationships*** with their clients, colleagues, professional allies, referral sources, influencers and communities of interest. It is this network that acts as their marketing engine and sales force—and that drives their success. It provides the repeat business, referrals, word of mouth advertising and business development leverage that is the lifeblood of a profitable law practice. *The bottom line is that their network is their most precious career asset.*

That is why we developed this course.

We will show YOU how to build a productive network of relationships—teaching you WHAT to do and HOW to do it. Believe us. The power and vitality of your network will be your most important practice-building asset in your legal career. Therefore, apply the lessons you learn in this course on a daily, weekly and monthly basis. Start to see your business grow by cultivating a set of "business partner" relationships with your clients, colleagues and professional allies.

THE LEARNING OBJECTIVE OF THIS COURSE IS FOR YOU TO:
1. *Thoroughly understand the most effective and productive ways to market yourself and your practice through network building*

2. *Create your own personalized network building plan*

3. *Execute successfully those specific ideas you decide upon*

4. *Positively impact the quality of your practice*

5. *Materially affect the profitability of your practice as you implement what you have learned*

The professional arena in general and the law profession in particular has changed dramatically since the 1980s.

The marketing of professional services, therefore, is a relatively new discipline, and I haven't found very much written or spoken on it that is germane to, or produces results for, the legal profession. Much is totally worthless in applicable terms, written by professors of business who have little or no practical experience in the real world.

In my never ending study and quest of mastery of this subject, I've found that most authors and speakers have borrowed principles that might work well in marketing tangible items (like soup or copy machines) and have made them over for marketing professional services.

My experiences, and the wisdom of the best business producers in the professions, indicate quite the opposite is true: Whatever works in marketing a tangible product may be the exact opposite of what works in marketing an intangible, professional service. We will fully explore this subject and you will come to a clear understanding of what it takes to market your services and your practice most effectively through network building.

We are indeed fortunate to have Mike Cummings as co-author of this course. I don't believe anyone knows more about the marketing of professional services than Mike does.

Mike will laugh and tell you that he came to me in the 1980s to learn how to sell professional services, but he's the one who taught me so much of what marketing is all about. Mike is a founding member of Arthur Andersen's headquarters marketing group 'way back in 1980. He was instrumental there in managing the marketing function for six and one-half years. Since 1986, Mike has worked with many professional firms, large and small, to improve their business development results.

Today, as the founders and "rainmakers" of numerous firms retire (or hope to), many see that their fellow partners and staff simply aren't interested in, or capable of, growing the business. In one Top 20 firm that was recently sold to another law firm, only a veritable handful of the partners brought in the majority of the work, and they were all in their fifties or early sixties. No wonder they gladly found someone to buy their practice.

Most firms are started and grown by entrepreneurs who did "Marketing" and "Sold" work in order to eat. Other "rainmakers" are proficient at self-promotion and selling their services because they innately know how to do it well and, therefore, enjoy it. These entrepreneurial types did such a good job of bringing in work that they had to hire others to help them with the workload. Customarily, those hired were not entrepreneurial by nature, but technicians—they became attorneys because they liked the law, not because they wanted to spend their careers and free time marketing and selling professional services.

Unfortunately, most business generators can't tell you systematically how they've marketed themselves or how they sell work. But, we have diagnosed how they do it. This course is a systematic, step-by-step approach to effectively use network building to market your services and your practice— by emulating the business development attitudes and aptitudes of the top producers.

FIRST, SOME BACKGROUND INFORMATION

I hate networking! By nature, I'm not what you would call a "people person." As an only child, my idea of a good time is to come home and find no other cars in the driveway. I like the peace and quiet that comes from solitude. Some people find being around other people energizing; I find it hard work and draining. Give me a good book, leave me alone and I'm happy. I became a CPA to "think" for a living. Can you relate to any of that?

I find that about 90% of the thousands of other professionals and attorneys that I've trained and interacted with all over the world are a lot like me: somewhat introverted, often shy and critical and cautious by nature. If we weren't professionals, we might have made great cabinetmakers. We're proud of our finished work product and tend towards perfection.

I remember my first day in public accounting. After working in outside sales for a few years and despising it, I went back to school at night to earn enough credits to sit for the CPA exam.

Immediately after passing it I joined a local CPA firm in the Chicago area. We were a "boutique" audit firm, specializing in not-for-profits and manufacturing companies. We were known for our excellent technical work and were marketed brilliantly by our managing partner who spent most of his time at Rotary, eating lunch at the University Club or investing time with his clients and referral sources.

On that first day in public accounting back in 1976, the managing partner sat me down in my very own office overlooking Lake Michigan and the Northwestern University campus. Imagine a junior with his own office. Our conversation went something like this:

Him:	Allan, welcome to our firm. We're delighted that you chose to join us. How do you like your office?
Me:	It's great, what a view. Thanks a lot!
Him:	Enjoy it today, because this may be the last time you'll see it for a long, long time.
Me:	Huh?
Him:	You see, in our firm, we believe in doing all of our work at the client's office. They perceive a much higher value when they see us actually working there and are much likelier to pay our fees. Also, we believe that being on the client's premises affords us the opportunity to keep our ears open and listen for other ways we can help the client and sell them additional work.
Me:	Sell?
Him:	Sure. In fact, if you ever expect to be considered for partner around here you're going to have to market yourself and build your own book of business.
Me:	Gee, they never said anything about that in school!
Him:	I'm surprised. That was the main reason we hired you—you had lots of experience in marketing and selling before you joined our firm.

What a shocker. Our managing partner was very much ahead of his time. I became a CPA so I never would have to market or sell anything to anyone ever again. I wanted to get as far away from customers and clients and people as I possibly could—that's why I was attracted to our profession. Sit me down behind a spreadsheet and leave me alone! And now I was going to have to market my services in order to move ahead in the firm.

I went out and made the mistakes most professionals make in building their personal networks. I went to the wrong places (in my case Chambers of Commerce), joined the wrong organizations, and then didn't know what to do when I got there. I was spending evenings and sometimes weekends with strangers, away from the family, and generating basically nothing. I was told to be patient, that building networks and generating "leads" takes time. I was taking actions that weren't productive and was frustrated and tired.

So, I began my life's quest: becoming good at something I was not good at—building a professional services business. I started applying my auditing skills and commenced interviewing people that I met as to how they became successful at building their practice. The information was slow in coming and quite generic. One man told me "I stood in the hallway of our office building and shook hands." Pardon me? Another said, "I knocked on doors and introduced myself." Great. I figured if I did that for about fifty years I might eventually bump into someone who had just received a notice from the IRS or something.

What I learned from those successful at marketing, I began to practice, flourish at, and incorporate into a systematic approach. Working with Mike Cummings was a giant leap forward. In this course, you'll have the combined benefit of our forty years of study and practice on this subject of "marketing" and it's most important component for a professional, building his or her network.

THE GOOD NEWS

In this course you'll first learn how to conduct a "personal audit." And we'll start with what you already have going for you and guide you by the hand to emulate the super-productive behavior of the best business generators, the "rainmakers," in our profession.

Ours is a systematic approach that may be the opposite of what you may perceive "marketing" or "networking" to be. It's designed to be time and energy effective, and is adjustable to your personal style.

This "audit" approach is intended for you to be in control of the overall process, not just jump in to activity for it's own sake.

A SPECIAL REQUEST

This is not a traditional marketing course about how to cold call and write brochures, etc. Some of the ideas may not be what you expect and may be new to you. Our goal is not to have you use all of your free time to pump flesh, spend a lot of money on ineffective contact-making, or hang out at social functions.

We only want to help you become highly effective at network building systematically and painlessly to produce many more clients and opportunities for business.

Therefore, I request you approach the course with an open mind. **Attorneys are highly intelligent people.** They also may tend to be quite suspicious and critical. They are good investigators and are generally always looking for what's wrong.

If you're going to approach this course with the mind of a skeptic, looking for faults, exceptions, what is wrong, and the things you don't agree with, cancel it right now. You won't get anything out of the course. I promise you we're only passing along everything we know about network building for attorneys THAT IS PROVEN TO WORK, OVER AND OVER AGAIN.

Nobody has ever done more research into what makes marketing work in the professions and then simplified and prioritized it for you.

Please! Look for what's right in this course, instead. **Look to see where you can apply some of the ideas;** not all of the ideas will be appropriate for you because this course was written for a wide audience.

We're the experts; let go of your already existing beliefs about personal network building and personal marketing. Let us guide you by the hand to success.

Be aware that Mike and I have helped thousands of professionals and hundreds of firms become much more successful over the last twenty-plus years. Let us coach you, too.

Study, enjoy, and become a rainmaker!

INTRODUCTION BY MICHAEL CUMMINGS

My career has paralleled the explosive growth of marketing in the professions. And it illustrates how marketing is now ingrained into the law business. I believe that business development is now central to being a successful, entrepreneurial attorney.

MARKETING'S GROWTH IN IMPORTANCE IN THE 1980S & 1990S

For the sake of perspective, I had the distinction of being the second person hired into the fledgling marketing group at Andersen Worldwide (Accenture, Arthur Andersen) headquarters back in 1980. My only training in marketing came from my MBA school instruction.

However, this lack of experience was a blessing in disguise as marketing for professional firms was a brand new field. At the time, there were no established methods for the marketing of professional services. So, we were essentially pioneers facing an uncharted frontier.

Back in 1980, marketing was almost a "dirty" word. It implied that unscrupulous hucksters, hustlers and promoters were somehow going to take over the professions. The first wave of advertising in the early 80s seemed to confirm this perception.

Throughout the 80s and 90s, law firms had to invent productive approaches as they went along—borrowing some techniques from the marketing of other services (like banking or financial services), modifying other business-to-business marketing techniques, analyzing the winning methods that their most successful partners employed to build the practice. Seeing our service through the eyes of our clients and prospects through market research and interviewing was also critical.

My tenure at Arthur Andersen & Co. lasted from 1980 through 1987. Over that time, my colleagues and I grew the marketing function from 3 people to a staff numbering over 35 professionals. By 1986, each office had designated a partner to be the marketing director—in most cases it was the managing partner. Also, every office had a full-time marketing specialist. Clearly, marketing was making a visible contribution to the success of our industry programs, consulting service areas and offices.

Now, marketing is a widely accepted, vital function at most top professional firms (including law). Other professions simply had a head start over law. For example, in 2003 Accenture invested more in ONE television advertisement than our ENTIRE marketing budget in the combined Arthur Andersen/Andersen Consulting firm 1986.

Look around the law profession today. Most leading law firms have a marketing specialist on staff—and the big firms have even larger staffs. Many of the top 20 firms now employ full-time business development people. Partners at the large firms are now evaluated highly on their business development performance. In fact, entrepreneurial, marketing-oriented managing partners are running top law firms, which adds significantly to the competitive intensity within the profession. We see this emphasis on business development filtering down to the smallest, progressive firms.

Simply put, marketing is here to stay. You can no longer rely on the economy to boost your business. Marketing is no longer an optional skill. Without question, effective marketing is now central to your success as an attorney.

Now, why did we write this book? I decided to leave Arthur Andersen in 1986 to start and build a consulting and training firm and partnered up with Allan Boress & Associates in the late 1980s.

In our line of work, we've been lucky to work with top law firms, leading service organizations and major consulting companies to improve their business development results.

Our experience ranges from market planning to the development of industry/service area marketing campaigns. Also, we're the premier training firm in the professions—specializing in sales, client relationship, total quality service, personal marketing—and *network building*.

So, everything that you'll learn in our business development series of courses—*I Hate Selling, I Hate Marketing* and *I Hate Losing Clients* has been tested and proven to work based on our association with all types of professional firms. (For details on these courses visit Allan's website: http://www.allanboress.com/training)

Because my professional background was honed at Arthur Andersen, you may find references to them throughout this material. Let's be very clear: Andersen was the most successful firm in the world up until the Enron debacle and they were forced out of business. The average Andersen partner made twice what their closest competitor did, and they were leap years ahead of the competition in creating successful professional services marketing.

I am extremely proud of my work with Arthur Andersen. You will learn from their successes and failures, as I did, during this course.

Let's Get Started.

But, it will only work for you if you are committed to building your network and your networking skill base. Like a technical skill, we've found that network building is a skill that you can improve if you work at it.

Now, there are time-tested and proven winning principles that attorneys can employ. And that's the point of the course. We want you to benefit from our 40 combined years of concentrated expertise in this field.

WHY MARKETING IS HERE TO STAY

In the past, you could almost hang out a shingle and business would come in across the transom. If you were a competent technician and diligent worker, you were likely to be a success.

Those days are over. Being technically excellent is not enough. Without business generation skills, new clients simply won't be able to find you. Your prospective clients are being consistently and aggressively courted by a number of firms.

So, marketing is now a requisite skill in the legal profession—you can't afford to ignore it. And it will become even more important in the future.

FIVE REASONS WHY MARKETING IS HERE TO STAY

Think about how the legal profession has changed over the past decade or so. It's been radically transformed. Here are a few of the permanent, pervasive shifts that we've seen and many of you have experienced:

1. *Intense Competition.* In many cities across the nation clients of law firms are being bombarded by "cold" sales calls, letters, speeches, articles, advertisements and other marketing activities. Every bit of business is precious—for example, big law firms are targeting the entrepreneur and small business clients of smaller firms. Larger firms want smaller clients; sort of like setting up a farm system for future large clients. Meanwhile, top firms are marketing a wide array of special services. High asset, wealthy individuals are being courted by financial planners, bankers, insurance agents and attorneys. So, it's tougher than ever to grab the attention and interest of these targets. What's the end result? Some major firms are no longer in business and lots of smaller practitioners are on the fringe.

2. *Technical Parity.* These days, there are plenty of qualified attorneys who possess the technical skills needed to serve clients. Through continuing education requirements and other support programs offered by the ABA & the state bar associations, technical competency is available to all practitioners. So, it's difficult to distinguish yourself as a technician—especially in the eyes of clients who lack technical sophistication.

3. *Tighter Margins.* There is a clearly downward pressure on fees. It's no secret that many firms "low-ball" their bids to get some client assignments. Beyond fee pressure, investments in training, salaries, reference materials and marketing are putting pressure on your bottom line. So, how do you fight back? How can you make sure that clients see and appreciate the value that you deliver? Through top-notch service and client marketing.

4. *Less Client Loyalty.* Clients are switching firms more than ever before. And even more clients are considering the possibility of switching. Why is this happening? First, aggressive marketing and selling is having an impact. Secondly, many clients may not see a tangible value in the services provided—so if you can have the same work done for a cheaper price

then why not switch? Again, top-notch service, quality control and effective relationship marketing are the tools you employ to foster and strengthen client loyalty.

5. *More and More Marketing and Sales Activity.* Because of all these business pressures, marketing and sales activity seems to intensify each year. As more marketing oriented practitioners mature in the profession, marketing campaigns proliferate. Sales people and sales managers are now fixtures at many of the most successful firms. Business development performance is now evaluated at firms to determine partner and promotion potential. Simply put, marketing is NOW central to success in the legal profession and the associated consulting and financial service operations.

WHAT'S THE GOOD NEWS?

So, the bad news is that marketing is here to stay. But, the good news is that marketing is a skill—one that you can systematically build and apply.

By investing in this course, you're already ahead of the game. You're looking forward to the future—taking the time to strengthen the entrepreneurial skills that you need to succeed. Others are still clinging to the past—ignoring the obvious impact that marketing has made on the profession.

Now, let's see how you can become more skilled at building your network to grow your practice.

EXERCISE 1-1

Please complete this exercise as a prelude for the next chapter.

1. *What effect has marketing had on your own personal book of business?*

_____

_____

_____

2. *What differences have you noticed in the ways your competitors are marketing now versus three years ago?*

_____

_____

_____

_____

_____

_____

CHAPTER 2

BIGGEST MISTAKES ATTORNEYS MAKE IN MARKETING THEIR PRACTICES

INTRODUCTION AND PURPOSE OF THIS CHAPTER

Since 1980, we've observed the mistakes of many attorneys in marketing themselves and their practices.

The purpose of this chapter is to identify the most common and critical errors these people make when they invest their priceless time, effort, energy and resources in marketing.

If you can avoid these errors, your marketing effectiveness will improve dramatically.

MISTAKE #1: BEING PASSIVE.

It's a fact: the great majority of attorneys effectively ignore marketing altogether.

They're too busy "getting the work out" to invest time, thought or (heaven forbid) money into marketing. Many of them use excuses like "Our work speaks for itself" or, "We build our practice the way we always have, through technical excellence." Or, "Marketing is demeaning to our profession." Sound like anyone you know?

Chances are, however, that you don't think that way much at all. You probably have an existing desire or interest in marketing or you wouldn't be talking this course. But there's many more of those reactive thinkers out there than you think, and here's good proof: In preparation for writing this course, we interviewed over 46 managing partners of law firms all over the country. Firms ranging in size from small, niche firms to the largest offices of major firms. We wanted to know what these firms were doing differently in order to deal with increased competition and a changing profession.

Here are the results:

Less than 35% of the firms we interviewed were really doing anything different regarding their marketing programs, being proactive in their personal marketing efforts, or even changing the way they did business with their clients from the year before. Some boast to their buddies, but few actually take action and make the changes needed to succeed. The consensus from our interviews was that the profession, as a whole, were "too busy" to worry about generating new business or changing the way they went to market. Some had hired "marketing people" and assumed the issues we discuss in this course were "taken care of."

That's great news for you! That's why we say, "There is very little competition." However, if your firm and your partners and staff aren't marketing your firm actively, you're not competition either. Is there competition? Of course there is. A lot of it and more coming in the future.

Yes, there are other firms that feed the same market that you do, but what are they doing to increase their business? Do they have a concerted effort or are there one or two of the same old people hustling business like they always have?

Perhaps there are firms that are actively soliciting your clients via mail or phone. What are you doing to counteract that?

Maybe there are firms or individuals who are dramatically undercutting your fees, virtually giving away their services. You may have lost clients to these people. But does everyone, or even almost everyone, buy legal services based on fees? WE'VE FOUND THAT NO MATTER WHAT PART OF THE COUNTRY YOU LIVE IN, HOW BADLY YOU HAVE BEEN HURT BY ECONOMIC CONDITIONS AND COMPETITION, PEOPLE DO NOT BUY FOR FEES ALONE.

Do you go to the cheapest dentist or doctor in town?

Sure, you have had clients hit in the past by recessions, but prospered, despite it. Why? Because they know how to go to market, how to sell effectively, and have the right relationships with their clients and referral sources. **In this course, we'll show you how to effectively go to market.**

Does that mean you won't run into people who are mostly concerned with fees, no matter how well you market? Of course not; it means that you will have the ability to attract the kind of client that you want, instead of having the marketplace tell you what it wants.

And you get to determine fees when you and your firm are heavily proactively marketing in the most effective manner!

Passive firms are SITTING DUCKS to their more aggressive competitors. If you haven't done much marketing in the past, now is a good opportunity, starting with this course, to get with the program.

MISTAKE #2: HAVING THE WRONG EXPECTATIONS OF MARKETING

Take a moment and think about this question before you answer it: What's the purpose of marketing a *tangible item* like a personal computer or an automobile?

To create a desire? To get the name out? To get product information into the hands of the buyer? To "build a reputation?"

NO!

The only purpose of marketing a <u>tangible item</u> is to sell it immediately! Right now! They want you to march into that dealership and buy their new Fuzzmobile this very minute! At the highest possible price! Whether you need it or not!

And you will buy the tangible item because of the *item*, itself.

How many of us have had to live through that humbling experience known as purchasing an automobile? If the dealer has the car you want, at the right price, are you going to buy it even if they aren't necessarily nice, or professional, with you? You either like the tie you're looking at in the store, or you don't. The personal interaction with the seller has less to do with the purchase than the item itself.

*But, that's not how people buy professional, intangible services. They are buying the **promise** of quality work, and favorable results.*

With an intangible professional service, there's nothing to see, hear, feel, and smell! What you market, sell and deliver is invisible.

Here's proof about the different way people buy intangible services vs. tangible items: Do you get a lot of telephone calls asking for legal services "out of the blue" where people want to buy right over the phone? Get a lot of walk-in traffic where people just march right in your office off of the street with their records, sort of like those quickie haircut places? Do your clients buy your legal services "right off of the shelf," with little interaction from you? Come on, we don't think so.

We need to take a solid look at what people are really buying when they purchase legal services— **THEY'RE BUYING YOU!** No matter what firm you work for, big name or no name, the ultimate decision to purchase is based on interaction with real human beings.

Yes, if you spend an absolute fortune on advertising and entertaining and "getting the word out," about five years from now, the community will more readily recognize the name of your firm. Name recognition doesn't come overnight, and inexpensively. But, all that will do, possibly, is open the door a little wider. You still will get hired, or not hired, after they meet you! There are a lot of easier and less costly ways to get your foot in the door, and we'll show them to you.

Don't ever forget this marketing axiom:

People buy other people, not firms.

"Branding" is a good idea, as it makes you and your firm more readily recognizable and memorable. It will probably get you more opportunities. BUT! It is not the major determining factor in getting the client.

No matter if you work for the best-known firm in town, or the oldest firm in town, or Moe, Larry & Curly, the ultimate decision to use a service provider is based on human interaction.

Perhaps in the past you, or one of your colleagues, have come back after losing a sales opportunity and explained it away saying that the prospective client wanted to go with a "bigger name firm," or something like that. Be careful. The reason stated for not doing business is often not the real reason. People don't like hurting other's feelings. That's the way we were brought up. So, the buyer makes up an excuse like: "Your fees are too high." Or, "We need to go with a bigger firm," to placate you. They probably won't tell you the real reason because they don't want confrontation.

Our experience as marketing consultants to the law profession is overwhelmingly convincing that BUSINESS IS BASED ON RELATIONSHIPS.

That's good news: you don't have to invest a fortune on marketing to be effective at it. You will, however, have to get involved in the marketing effort and be willing to carry out the actions learned in this course.

And many firms think that if they conduct one seminar or run an ad, they're going to get business from it. Sorry, that's not how it works (although you could get lucky, conceivably).

Please don't forget this marketing axiom, either:

"Marketing is a process, not an event."

Marketing is a cumulative process, like a hurricane. Each marketing effort builds on what you've done in the past. One-shot marketing events rarely produce business—save your money and your time.

MISTAKE #3: BEING UNENLIGHTENED AS TO WHAT WORKS AND INVESTING IN USELESS MARKETING TOOLS

In this course we'll clue you in to what works.

MISTAKE #4: DOING "ME-TOO" PERSONAL MARKETING

Does your marketing look like everyone else's? Do you do the same kinds of marketing that your competitors do?

Marketing is one very important way you can separate yourself from the competition. "Me-Too" marketing dilutes your message and could send prospective clients to your rivals.

"Me-too" marketing also tends to be quite boring. Avoid uninteresting marketing—attorneys need to garner as much attention, in a professional manner of course, as possible because the very nature of our business can be construed by the public as not necessarily fascinating nor even that important.

MISTAKE #5: NOT MARKETING TO YOUR OWN CLIENTS

A good percentage of your new, incremental business must come from your existing clients and their referrals. Yet, most firms ignore their own clients when it comes to offering them new or additional services and treat their clients like "annuities" who they think won't go away because they are good attorneys and service providers.

In order to have a "healthy" marketing practice, here's where we believe new business should come from based on our experience with the individuals and firms who really do it right:

- *50% or so of new business needs to come form your existing clients AND their referrals*

- *25–35% or so of new business needs to come from "referral sources" such as attorneys, bankers, insurance agents, real estate people, your friends and relatives, firm alumni, investment bankers, business brokers, other attorneys and consultants, etc.*

- *About 20–25% should come from "strangers" via seminars, articles, speaking engagements, advertising, direct mail, etc.*

What if you're new to the area? What if you don't have a lot of contacts? What if you're new to the profession? What if you are in a purely transaction-based practice?

Well, you may have to increase the 25% way out of proportion. We'll teach you everything you need to know about how to parlay your existing resources and pursue "outside" forms of marketing.

Most firms look to take the easy way out, by marketing to the "25% strangers" through direct mail, advertising or looking for the proverbial "silver bullet" that will magically provide business for them, instead of emphasizing face-to-face contact making.

Marketing Rule:
Marketing is a Contact Sport

The point is that most firms ignore their own backyard. Then, they are surprised when outside resources wind up selling services to the firm's existing clients that could be provided by the firm. After interviewing over 600 large and small clients of law firms for this course, we discovered that most don't even know what other services their attorneys can perform for them.

Worse, it's those outside resources that your clients use, instead of you, that infect the client relationship. Once you have an outside resource doing work for your client, the relationship is now at risk because sharp service providers try to bring their buddies into your client relationship. It secures their position and pays back referrals received.

It's also important to continue to market to your clients to let them know how valuable you are— why using you is such a good idea. One reason auto companies advertise so heavily is because they want additional purchases from their existing customers and referrals. They constantly drive home the value of their product as they know it's much more difficult to attract business from someone who has never done business with them before than to keep and get more business from someone they already have in their stable as a customer.

Much of the growth and profitability of firms that are extremely successful is due to the additional or follow-on services sold to existing clients, often on a value-billing basis.

MISTAKE #6: IGNORING INTERNAL MARKETING

All of the marketing in the world, no matter how great it is, won't be nearly as effective if everyone isn't on the bandwagon back at the firm. Successful firms involve everyone in marketing the firm's services.

Did you know that everyone in your firm is conveying a message all of the time to everybody about your firm? That's the essence of marketing. How is your phone answered? What do your work products look like? What does your office look like? What do your people look like? Are they dressing 'business casual' or 'homeless casual?' How do they treat your clients? What message are you trying to convey, but aren't?

If your firm and your people aren't in alignment with the kind of client you're trying to attract, marketing can't work.

Everyone in the firm needs their own "personal marketing plan." Even the receptionist. Everyone needs to know what's expected of him or her as his or her part of the marketing effort.

MISTAKE #7: SEARCHING FOR TOO MANY REFERRAL SOURCES

As we said earlier, a significant portion of your new business, about 25%, needs to come from referral sources, outside of clients. What if your percentages differ from ours? You may be doing something very right (e.g.: getting a lot of new work from clients) but ignoring your referral relationships.

Most attorneys don't understand what it takes to have a true referral relationship. We'll discuss that later. Most attorneys also look at referral relationships as a numbers game: "The more people I know, the more people who will send me business!" Not necessarily. The Best Business Generators in the accounting and legal professions most often have FEWER, but far better referral sources than their less productive rivals.

MISTAKE #8: MARKETING TO TOO MANY DIFFERENT MARKETS

We often start consulting engagements with discussions about exactly what kind of new business the firm would want. What's interesting about attorneys in particular is, they want everything! Contract work—sure! We'd love some of that! Keep our people busy. Not-for-profit work? Sure, let's get some of that! Privately held companies? Definitely! E-commerce? Oh yeah!

Most law firms use the "Chinese Menu" approach to marketing: You want it? We got it! If that diluted approach works for you and your firm, keep using it. We find repeatedly, though, that many firms invest a lot of money and effort into marketing technical expertise that nobody cares about. We see many firms pursue markets they shouldn't, thus diluting the overall marketing effectiveness.

Now, we don't want to downplay the importance of technical expertise as the foundation for all good marketing. But you have to know what kind of technical expertise the market and client wants before you market it. The best example of this is 'web-trust.' So many firms have invested a lot of time, money and effort with minimal or no results because they were pushing an expertise, that nobody in that business really wanted or was going to pay for.

Also, promoting to markets where you don't already have a presence can be a long and difficult road. Later we'll discuss the concept of "cloning" your best clients.

MISTAKE #9: LACK OF DAY-TO-DAY CONSISTENCY AND PERSISTENCE

On what day does Toyota not advertise? Christmas? New Year's? Somebody recently said "December 7th" (for you Generation X'ers, that's the day the Japanese bombed our installation at Pearl Harbor and was the start of the US' involvement in World War II)? Nope. Toyota advertises every single day.

As we said earlier, marketing is a process, not an event. Marketing needs to be conducted even during your most busy time, to be most effective. Otherwise, you have to get all geared up all over again and almost start from scratch whenever the case is over.

There is time in everyone's day to go to market: it's called lunch (or breakfast, or dinner), downtime or commuting time. Most people eat lunch, even when busy. However, we usually eat lunch by ourselves or at our desks or with our friends at the firm.

We suggest not less than two lunches or breakfasts or after-work meetings a week with clients, referral sources, prospective clients, etc. even during busy season. The attorneys who are committed to successful marketing don't leave the marketplace when busy. Many increase their exposure because they know that when they are busy with clients it is simply the best time of the year to do marketing.

MISTAKE #10: BEING CHEAP

How much do your most successful clients spend promoting their businesses? What would happen if they stopped?

It seems to us that almost every attorney wants to save as much money as possible. The great majority of attorneys don't see the difference between marketing costs and investments.

The most successful firms we know set aside a percentage of gross revenues and treat it as a fixed cost, like rent, to do marketing. Perhaps the most successful firm in the country that we know invests 8% of gross revenues in marketing. In the beginning, that percentage was higher for them. The most successful accounting firm we know of invests 10% of gross revenues in marketing. Few law firms invest more than 3–5%, and usually that includes non-marketing items buried there by the partners.

Similarly, most firms and individuals don't take the skills of personal marketing and selling seriously enough, nor are they willing to invest in their people to properly prepare the partners and staff to succeed at bringing in more business. Less than 10% of the major firms in the US provide material business development training to their people in this area and then they wonder why they lose golden opportunities, get beat up on fees, or simply don't generate enough golden opportunities in the first place.

Folks, get over yourself and your ego. They didn't teach you how to market and sell your services in the Harvard Business School. Marketing and selling are the greatest skills in the world, one that can be learned. Look at analogous fields. Consider Bill Clinton. His people did a great job of "marketing" his presidency. Bill Clinton was a beautifully "packaged" candidate and left office with one of the highest ratings of any president as they continued to market to their customers even after the sale was made.

"Running for office" can be quite similar to "Personal Marketing for Attorneys," or "Running for Expert". It's a person-to-person event. Some people are born with personal marketing skills, but most attorneys aren't (and that's a good reason why they became legal professionals instead of salespeople).

So, to amplify the productivity of your firm's marketing efforts, involve your people, you included, in as much marketing and selling skill development as you possibly can.

Marketing is an Investment, not a Cost!

MISTAKE #11: RELYING ON THE MARKETING PEOPLE TO DO ALL OF THE WORK

Over time, some firms have hired "marketing directors" to handle the marketing chores. These professionals are likely the most frustrated people we know.

Almost every single law firm we've ever talked to that has allocated someone to the marketing function (sometimes a clerical person with no real knowledge or background in marketing)—and expected them to be the only ones to bring in business—has been disappointed.

NO! That's not how it works! If marketing and generating new business worked that way, every firm would be on that bandwagon. And your business development people wouldn't need you

Everyone must be involved in the marketing effort! The partners can't pass it on to the staff and to the marketing person. *All marketing does is provide the opportunity.* Good marketing puts you in the position to get that opportunity more often than the competition. Somebody still has to show up and get the work (that's called 'selling')! The biggest complaint I hear from marketing directors is: "I can't get our people to do anything."

MISTAKE #12: NOT QUICKLY OR THOROUGHLY FOLLOWING THROUGH ON THE LEADS GENERATED BY MARKETING

Good leads are hard to come by for most of us. People that don't follow through on marketing leads should be ashamed of themselves. We've found that its the same people who complain about not enough new business, are the ones who don't jump on referrals and hot leads immediately before they cool off. The longer one waits to follow through on that referral or interest shown by a prospective or existing client, the colder that lead gets and the harder to convert into business.

Yes, you do have time to follow through on leads—it's called lunch. In the following chapters we'll address these mistakes and their accompanying cures, in detail.

EXERCISE 2-1

1. *What is "Marketing?"*

_____

_____

_____

2. *What is "Selling?"*

_____

_____

_____

3. *How does "Marketing" differ from "Selling?"*

_____

_____

_____

4. *What is the purpose of marketing a tangible item, like a computer?*

_____

_____

_____

5. *What is the purpose of marketing an intangible professional service?*

_____

_____

_____

CHAPTER 3

WHAT 'MARKETING' IS
AND HOW IT DIFFERS FROM 'SELLING'

INTRODUCTION AND PURPOSE OF THIS CHAPTER

Let's take a look at what the marketing and selling of professional services is in the real world of business development as opposed to what you may have read in textbooks and other preconceived notions you bring into this course (which may or may not be correct). We will reflect upon your answers from the previous exercise and introduce some new definitions.

The purpose of this chapter is to immerse you in the concept of what marketing professional services successfully really is.

MARKETING DEFINED

After twenty years of studying, learning, applying, analyzing, adapting and consulting on the subject, here's our definition of marketing professional services:

> *Marketing is ANYTHING that puts YOU in front of a PERSON that you want to do business with.*

This definition frees you up to be creative and acknowledges that any contact you have with clients, prospective clients and referral sources is "MARKETING." The key word in that last sentence is **"CONTACT."** (Don't forget: your current clients should be a powerful source of new business through the purchasing of additional services and their referrals).

> *Marketing is a Contact Sport!*

Marketing should be considered as any kind of interaction that you or your firm has between clients, prospective clients, non-clients, referral sources, prospective referral sources, recruits, EVERYBODY (including salespeople, the Xerox repairman, the postal service person—anyone who steps into or calls your office or comes into contact with you or your people).

Every contact must be considered "marketing": telephone conversations, work products, work done at the client's office, how your people look and act, etc. YOU ARE ALWAYS MARKETING YOURSELF whether you think so or not. The people who work for you are always marketing the firm and themselves whether they know it (or care) or not. Marketing is broadcasting; its very essence is communication.

You and your firm are always sending messages out into the world, and inside your own office, which affect whether or not your firm is perceived the way you want it to be and may determine whether you get enough of the kinds of opportunities you want.

Everything about you and your firm broadcasts a message. What does your office look like? Carpets dirty or old? Walls banged up? Are your stationery, business cards and web site affecting the kind of image you want to project to attract the kind of client and referral source and business that you want? How do your people treat the clients and everyone who comes in contact with your firm? How is your phone answered? Do clients feel like long lost relatives with money when they call or might they feel like strangers or taken for granted? Can they even understand the name of the firm when the phone is answered?

Every person your firm comes in contact with knows about 250 people—their own personal network. When you think of powerful marketing, remember that you're broadcasting not to individuals, but potentially to that number of individuals times 250.

(As an aside, we've determined that 250 is a good number from interviewing funeral home directors and caterers. On the average 250 people or so show up for someone's funeral. Also, we've talked to caterers—given that they could afford it, the average bride and groom would invite about 250 people each.)

Case studies have proven that people tell ten other people on the average when they've had a negative experience with a business or service provider but tell only three other people when the experience is positive.

YOU'RE AN EXPERIENCED MARKETEER

If you look at our definition "Marketing is anything that puts you in front of someone you want to do business with" in a positive light, you can now see that you've been marketing quite a bit all along (but perhaps not realizing it). Now you have the opportunity to shift that marketing to create the results you want.

Every contact you have is "marketing." You are now totally free to create your own "marketing." But, marketing is a contact sport—the quality of the marketing not only depends on the image or messages produced and received but ALSO ITS QUALITY AND FREQUENCY. The more frequent the contact, the more likely the opportunity to have others purchase your services. "Out of sight, out of mind" is an axiom that applies directly to who gets the referrals and hot leads.

This is proven time and again by the firm that provides recurring annual work or sporadic engagements but has little or no face-to-face contact (or much other type of contact) with the client the rest of the year. As an example, we've seen on repeated occasions where a firm walks in the following year to do some expected work only to discover that the client has addressed a legal need without even thinking about their firm. Quite frequently, the firm could've (and should've) been able to help out, thereby losing additional billable hours and causing the infection of an outside intruder into the relationship.

Why do these things happen? Lack of proper marketing (the client may not even know you can offer the service) and lack of face-to-face and other contact. It is essential to let the client know what you can offer and to keep yourself in front of the client for when the opportunity presents itself.

The above example equally applies to the attorney who regularly and consistently services, but has little direct contact with, the client. Some people don't even see their clients, conducting business through the mail or Internet. Saves time? Yes. Bad marketing? Yes.

PUTTING MARKETING IN PERSPECTIVE

All excellent marketing of professional services can be expected to do is provide more opportunities, not complete the actual sale of the item.

The purpose of marketing a tangible item is to create the desire in the prospective buyer that motivates them to buy the product (off of the shelf) right now, for as much money as possible and with as little interference from the salesperson as possible. This explains why mass merchandisers and supermarkets changed retailing. They eliminated the least important part of the equation in buying their items: the human being. No matter how much you like and respect the salesperson, if the tangible product (i.e.: the coat or the computer) isn't right for you, you just won't buy it.

Yes, given similar tangible products, like gas pumps sold to refineries, the last determining factor in the purchase may well be the relationship between the purchasing agent and the salesperson. But, if that's the right pump, it'll be purchased despite the relationship—the material item is in the spotlight. Of course post-purchase servicing by the manufacturer is an important consideration, but, unless the item is similar to others or generic, it can be less important in the decision than the item itself.

Let's face it: If it's the right car, dress or computer, you're going to buy it despite the manner in which you are treated the vast majority of the time.

WHAT YOU ARE REALLY MARKETING

The marketing of legal services adds and emphasizes something completely different from the consequences of the provided service itself. In promoting legal services, all we have to market and sell as attorneys is US!

No matter what firm you work for, people buy other people; they buy into the individuals they interact with. This explains why you may at times lose business to less qualified firms. Your prospective buyer often has no point of reference or expertise in the area of service you are promoting.

Marketing Rule:
Since <u>you</u> are the product,
you must market you

One of our first consulting projects in training attorneys how to sell and market their services came from the managing partner of an international firm, after they had just lost the largest client in the entire country to a large local firm based in a major city.

Interestingly, the firm that lost the client is known in the industry as a very good technical firm. The local firm that won the client is not.

___

Here's what happened:

> The managing partner of the local firm met the CEO of the client eight years earlier and began cultivating a relationship with the client. ***(Business is relationships).*** He met with the CEO on a regular basis to see how things were going, took him out to lunch, joined the same clubs, sent him articles, took him to ball games, etc. You get the picture. (Please remember that this is the biggest client of an international firm—a jewel of a prize that would be worth the effort).

> Six years later, the partner in charge of the client (from the old firm) retired. He had enjoyed an excellent relationship with the CEO (which is a good reason why the CEO didn't switch in those years despite being "romanced" by the other attorney). This partner was replaced by a junior partner who had little or no contact or, relationship, with the client. (An obvious mistake, you say? Happens all of the time).

> Even small firms regularly replace key people without regard for the lack of existing relationship with the client, and then ignore ways to build that relationship. Why? Because most professionals see the most important part of the client relationship as being the technical work done, e.g.: the case, contract or advice, rather than the relationship between client and legal service provider.

> Two years later, in the eighth year of pursuit, the managing partner of the local firm reeled in the biggest fish of his career: the largest client of an international firm.

This theory of how people buy intangible professional services vs. tangible items also accounts for why you do not often have people buy major legal services over the phone with their credit cards.

Because our services are "invisible" and sometimes considered generic, many firms go out of their way to distinguish themselves from the competition. The concept of "Branding" is a hot topic today. Still, the decision to purchase is made upon interaction with the service provider (or who they think will be the service provider) and the buyers.

PERCEPTION IS REALITY

Recently we had a client relate to us that she had visited an attorney's office to get him involved with the local community center. She, not an attorney, was not impressed. Why? His office had nothing on the walls, no pictures, no citations, no diplomas, no books, nothing (no, he had not just moved in). Her reaction, that of a potential client, and a potential referral source, was that he wasn't a competent attorney! The visual effect of his office (or lack thereof) had that negative outcome on her judgment and her influence on the 250 people she knows.

___

Every single interaction you have must be considered MARKETING.

You are always broadcasting a message, so be careful about what communication you are sending and its intended effect.

Therefore, is "billing" marketing? Yes. Some firms send out bills that read "January services: $5,000." Other firms, who we have determined, have less fee resistance (by interviewing their clients), send out completely detailed billings describing the work performed for the client. One of our law firm clients details the client benefit, line item by line item. Outrageous? Yes. Time consuming? Yes. Adds value in the client's eyes? **Absolutely**. The client now sees what she is getting. And their fees are at least 25% higher than their competitors for the same kind of work, and they are certainly no more competent or expert at law than their rivals are.

You and your firm are always sending messages into the world that affect whether or not your firm is perceived the way you want it to be and may determine whether you get enough of the kinds of opportunities you want.

LEARN ABOUT THE VALUE OF CONTACT FROM THE PROS

In 1993, the Clinton administration put into motion a plan of emulating The Great Communicator (Ronald Reagan, who left office with the highest rating of any president in 150 years). Clinton administration officials resurrected the "message of the day"—a daily planned media message that Reagan mastered and the next president, George Bush, ignored. Additional ideas put in place were the wide use of satellite feeds to local TV stations, an electronic mail system accessible to the public by personal computer, and daily faxes and phone calls to key media friends from the White House.

In 1993 *The Wall Street Journal* reported that the Clinton administration wanted to circumvent and supplement the national news media with direct feeds to local stations and make the new president available to local TV stations (personalizing the message for your buyer) for interviews with local TV anchors.

Clinton's administration said it wanted to "open the doors and open the windows of the White House and give the American people the opportunity to know what is going on every day." (Communication is the very essence of marketing professional services.)

Clinton's team, borrowing heavily from Reagan's strategy, planned a two-prong approach to keep his popularity high: to neutralize enemies and keep positive images before the public. They wanted to convey the image that Mr. Clinton was unusually open, when in reality (according to the Wall Street Journal) he often "bristles when the news media wants to cover him jogging or golfing."

Was the Clinton administration successful? He left office with the highest rating of any sitting president, despite many personal problems that were intensely covered by the national media.

LEARN FROM YOUR PEERS ABOUT CONTACT

"Joe," one of the country's most successful attorneys, regularly makes rounds with his doctor clients. No time for that you say? Here's a guy who's managing a practice several times larger than the typical lawyer's. He finds the time.

"Betty," partner in a national firm, goes jogging every morning with her best clients and referral sources.

"Jim," managing partner of one of the nation's largest independent firms works out at the club with his clients, referral sources and power brokers in the city.

Do these people have the time to make this contact? They *make* time, and that's how they've become so phenomenally successful, because they know that "marketing" is anything you do that puts you in front of people you want to do business with. And, that frequency of contact is the very essence of successful marketing. Business is relationships. People buy other people; they don't buy "firms."

---

*It's the <u>quantity</u> of contact you have
with clients, targeted clients and referral
sources that is important because this
establishes the personal chemistry needed
to improve the <u>quality</u> of the contact.*

WHAT YOU SHOULD EXPECT FROM MARKETING AND WHAT WORKS

The most effective marketing we have ever found that produces winning results on a consistent basis is personal marketing, and it's principal component network building. Wherever you go, you will find business if you know how to personally market yourself.

Yes, there are instances where direct mail marketing, advertising, speeches, etc. produce good results. Those instances are driven by the situation: what is being marketed, where and to whom. These kinds of marketing are known as "institutional marketing" and are designed to magnify your personal marketing, not replace it.

If you're looking in this course for some "silver bullet" that will solve all of your business development problems, like a magic advertisement, forget it. If there were such a thing, others would find out about it (like us, who interact with thousands of professional service providers every year) and everyone would be using it, and it would become useless.

One reason personal marketing is so successful in getting new business and keeping clients, is that so few (relatively) of your peers do it in a systematic, daily basis and fewer do it well.

Excellent marketing can only provide the opportunity more often, which is called "POSITIONING." That is, being in the right position to get that great opportunity when it avails itself (rather than having your competitor get it).

No matter how great the marketing, though, people still have to be "sold" (or converted into a client) by a human being. Superb marketing (personal and otherwise) can pre-dispose the prospective client to hire you, but that doesn't mean you have the sale sewn up.

Many attorneys have become disenchanted with marketing because they expected business to happen simply by hiring a marketing director, by advertising, by distributing handsome brochures, from their web site, from "branding," or from direct mail as it does for marketing soup or television sets. Sadly, all marketing can be expected to do for us is provide the opportunity.

Excellent marketing provides many more opportunities than you may now currently enjoy, thus greatly increasing your chances of getting more clients.

Doing the wrong marketing can be time consuming, disappointing and wasteful of precious resources. We've seen firms squander tens of thousands of dollars (in one instance, over a million dollars) on seminars and other marketing efforts with no results at all!

We know of one firm that invested ("wasted" is more like it) over $100,000 on a six-month radio campaign that resulted in four phone calls and no new business. And one of those calls was from us because we wanted to know why they were doing so much advertising!

BEWARE OF CONFLICTING MARKETING MESSAGES

Bear in mind that conflicting marketing, such as promoting an image of care and proactivity with ideas, can be lethal if your people don't live up to that image.

We know of one firm that generated a ton of word-of-mouth advertising in their community by working up a marketing campaign surrounding client service, care and "partnership" with their clients' businesses.

Only one problem: they had poor client service, they didn't know much at all, nor care, about their clients' businesses, had high turnover, and they had little face-to-face contact (a.k.a. "personal marketing") with their clients. Net result: attention attracted for all of the wrong reasons. They sent forth an image that had no basis in fact and it got people talking, all right—negatively.

Couldn't happen to your firm, you say? How do you know? Have you conducted a TRUE client survey recently?

'MARKETING' VERSUS 'SELLING'

It is important to create a distinction between marketing legal services and selling legal services because they are very different in purpose. We don't want to expect results from marketing that can only be accomplished through active selling.

Most attorneys confuse marketing with selling. The truth is that law schools concentrate mostly on the technical skills necessary to be a good service provider. Very few schools, if any, teach you how to run your legal practice, how to build it, how to communicate better with your clients, how to keep your clients happy (besides the technical aspects), how to win friends and influence people, how to manage your employees (and fellow partners—now there's a challenge!). You get the idea.

In order to be better at marketing, and get excellent results, you must know exactly what the differences are between marketing and selling.

"Marketing" gets you there. "Selling" is what you do once you get there to convert the prospect into a client.

THE FIRST STEP

The very first step in marketing professional services most effectively (or marketing anything for that matter) is to put yourself in the shoes of the buyer. In order to be a successful marketer, you must stop looking at the world through the eyes of an attorney and start looking at the world through the eyes of your buyer.

Who Is Your Buyer?

Is your typical buyer an entrepreneurial type of person? A business owner perhaps? A corporate executive? Or are the only potential buyers you ever come in contact with fellow attorneys, like yourself?

Have you noticed that entrepreneurial/leader types tend to think and act differently than the typical attorney? What drives the business owner or executive? The details of your project or results? Aren't business owners and executives (the successful ones, that is) more similar to Colin Powell, Hillary Clinton, and Bill Parcells (the famous football coach)?

Aren't entrepreneurs/leaders most interested in winning and producing results? Is that what attorneys tend to be like?

How is the Decision to be Made?

Have you also noticed that "leader" types make many decisions that aren't as logical as you would? Or, that many of these people ignore the most rudimentary principles in running their business, like paying strict attention only to the numbers? That they often make decisions based more on emotion than logic?

Put yourself in the shoes of the buyer before you do any kind of marketing or selling. Remember that what *you* would look for in an attorney (in your area of expertise) is most likely totally different that what your pro-typical prospective client is looking for.

Imagine instead, how you make decisions to hire a dentist, or an auto mechanic (two areas of life that you may not be an expert at). Do you go to the cheapest doctor in town? The cheapest dentist? The cheapest auto mechanic? Highly unlikely. Do you shop six dentists before you select one to work on your mouth? That's doubtful.

Perhaps you're saying to yourself right now that the authors of this course don't know what they're talking about—that you work and practice in a distressed area and/or with extreme competition cutting fees constantly. But do all of the prospective clients and clients in your marketplace buy only on fees and want the bare minimum done for their businesses?

Our experience says "no." We have clients who have been highly successful even in hard times, because they knew what they were REALLY marketing and what their buyers REALLY wanted (without spending a fortune on advertising or marketing). Does that mean that people aren't interested in fees? Does that imply that there aren't buyers out there whose primary motive is to pay as little as possible? Of course not. You just have to get in front of the ones who are most interested in results and will be willing to pay your fees.

How? Through effective, targeted personal marketing, focused on solving a client's "pain."

As we embark on this journey towards highly successful marketing of professional services, *you must get rid of your preconceived notions of what works and doesn't* in marketing and trust us to lead you. We believe that "normal" human beings hire attorneys for different reasons than you would in the same situation. If you do all of the exercises in this book, if you study it (and not just read it) and put the ideas into action, IF YOU GIVE MARKETING YOUR ABSOLUTE BEST SHOT, then you can yell at us and you will have succeeded in proving that we are wrong. Until then, put yourself always in the shoes of the buyer first, in order to be more successful at marketing.

THE PRACTICE DEVELOPMENT PROCESS

In order to understand precisely where marketing fits into the business development process, here's a synopsis of how practice development works for all professional service firms:

1. *Prospective clients need to be put into what's known as a "marketing funnel" (see exhibit 3-1).* This is done through "marketing" such as personal contact, networking, advertisements, referrals, etc.

2. *Once in the "funnel," these people need to be "sold" or converted into clients.* Some will become clients, some won't. (Reference the "I-Hate-Selling Book" or "I-Hate-Selling Tapes" available at http://www.ihateselling.com)

3. *Those that do become clients fall into our "client base."*

4. *Once in your client base, you want to keep as many of the good ones as possible and avoid "leakage" (reference our "I-Hate-Losing-Clients Course").*

5. *Since the environment is a popular topic these days, we want to "recycle" these clients to buy additional services and get their referrals.* (Reference all three courses)

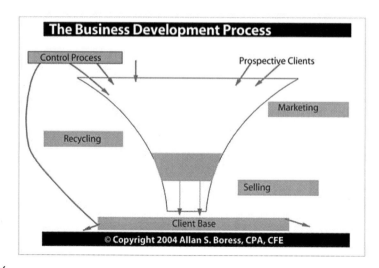

SUMMARY

In this chapter we have discussed what the marketing and selling of professional services is:

- Marketing is anything that puts you in front of someone you want to do business with.

- All you have to really market is YOU.

- The first step in successful marketing is to put yourself in the shoes of the buyer.

- "Good" marketing leads to "a personal value proposition" which puts you in the situation to get more of your share of opportunities.

- Marketing professional services provides the opportunity to sell.

- You and your firm are always marketing, whether you realize it or not.

- Beware of conflicting marketing messages.

EXERCISE 3-1

Kindly complete this exercise in preparation for the next chapter.

Pretend that you have just received notification from your spouse that they want a divorce.

Because you have worked so very hard to build a substantial practice and have significant equity in your home and possess other valuable assets, you are properly concerned that your assets are protected.

Now you need a divorce attorney. Describe, in step-by-step sequence, how you will determine who to represent you in this case:

Step #1: _____

Step #2: _____

Step #3: _____

Step #4: _____

Step #5: _____

BUILDING YOUR PERSONAL NETWORK

AN OVERVIEW

As we noted earlier, *the top rainmakers see themselves as experts in the relationship business*. Simply put, the top producers have consciously and systematically built a *comprehensive network of vital relationships* with their clients, colleagues, professional allies, referral sources, influencers and communities of interest. It is this network that acts as their marketing engine and sales force—and that drives their success. It provides the repeat business, referrals, word of mouth advertising and business development leverage that is the lifeblood of a profitable law practice. *The bottom line is that their network is their most precious career asset*—and the key to a successful career for any practicing attorney.

That is why we developed this course.

We will show YOU how to build a productive network of relationships—teaching you WHAT to do and HOW to do it. Believe us. The power and vitality of your network will be your most important practice-building asset in your legal career. Therefore, apply the lessons you learn in this course on a daily, weekly and monthly basis. Start to see your business grow by cultivating a set of "business partner" relationships with your clients, colleagues and professional allies.

What is PRODUCTIVE network building?

- *Finding people who are qualified to help you build your practice*

- *A "sorting-out process"*

- *Building a set of business partners that act as your marketing engine and personal sales force*

- *Creating a wealth of word-of-mouth advertising and steady referral stream of "pre-sold" prospective clients*

- *Finding innovative ways to mutually co-market and sell with your professional allies*

- *Creating mutually rewarding business and personal relationships*

- *Cultivating a life-long, career-building asset*

These chapters guide you through the best approach to building your personal network in a step-by-step manner. This approach has been proven to work for the top rainmakers in the legal profession.

It covers much more than what is commonly considered "networking." For it starts with your top priorities and opportunities, namely clients and referral sources and then moves outward—a true "inside-out" process. The objective—always—is to build a productive network, not spend time on ineffective networking.

HERE'S WHAT YOU WILL LEARN:

Chapters 4 and 5 help you establish your mind set toward marketing and network building—as well as your FOCUS, the essential set of priorities for any network building or personal marketing.

Chapters 6 through 9 take you through the essential components of a productive network building program from the "inside-out," with Chapter 9 summing up what you need to do and taking the ideas a step further.

Then Chapters 10 and 11 detail two of the best ways to energize your network building activities.

In each chapter we will show you what to do and how to do it. Put this system to work and see the results.

THE NETWORK BUILDING PROGRAM:

Chapter 4:	Lessons Of The Best Business Generators
Chapter 5:	How To Focus On Your Best Opportunities
Chapter 6:	Marketing To Your Existing Clients
Chapter 7:	Building Alliances
Chapter 8:	Obtaining High Quality Referrals
Chapter 9:	Creating Word Of Mouth Advertising
Chapter 10:	Building Your Reputation Through Public Speaking
Chapter 11:	Building Your Reputation By Writing Articles

LESSONS FROM THE BEST BUSINESS GENERATORS IN THE PROFESSIONS

INTRODUCTION AND PURPOSE OF THIS CHAPTER

In our consulting and training work, we've had the good fortune to work with some of the top business producers in the legal profession over the past twenty years.

With this close association and continuing working relationship with those that excel at business development, we've enjoyed a unique opportunity to share ideas, confirm success strategies, test marketing methods and understand how they excel.

Right now, we want to share the step-by-step approach that allows the best business generators to surpass the results that others achieve. Why?

BECAUSE YOU WANT TO PRODUCE THE SAME RESULTS. That's your goal. That's what marketing and business development are all about. Too often, attorneys think the answer to effective marketing comes down merely to better marketing tools—like public relations, seminars, advertising, brochures, logos, web sites and direct mail.

That kind of marketing is meaningless without the proper foundation. Look at what distinguishes the best individual business generators from the others. They don't aim to have the best marketing. Simply put, the critical difference comes down to their entrepreneurial behavior and the quality of their personal marketing effort. Study the best business generators that you know and you'll find that their SUCCESS ISN'T ACCIDENTAL. There are specific skills, attitudes, behavior, daily habits and patterns of action that lead to results.

The purpose of this chapter is to coach you towards building your personal success strategy and action plan—by "modeling" or emulating the behavior of the best business generators. Here's another way to look at it. In this chapter, you'll be mentored by the top producers in the profession. You'll benefit by seeing what it takes to produce the top-notch results you desire—from the professionals who are already generating a substantial base of business.

Our goal is to make it easy for you to grasp these principles and then quickly apply them to your practice. To this end, we've simplified and systematized the lessons and proven practices of the best business generators, so, in effect, you can use this system as a blueprint for building your own practice.

PUT MARKETING TOOLS IN THEIR PROPER PERSPECTIVE

Think about marketing this way: Marketing tools are simply equipment—like a golf club is to a golfer. Getting the best clubs money can buy will not make you shoot par. Lowering your score or becoming a pro depends primarily on your skill as a golfer. And that comes from dedicated, continual application of what works.

Also, remember that most marketing that you're familiar with isn't appropriate for legal services. Many attorneys make expensive mistakes by trying out marketing approaches that work for computers, copying machines and soap. This kind of product-oriented marketing simply is a waste of time.

So, what's the answer? Believe this: If you want to get better results, you must find ways to become more like the best business generators. Adopt their proven approaches to building your practice. Skillfully emulate their behavior and consistently practice their tactics on a daily basis.

What can you expect if you follow this advice? You'll find that getting better at business development is fully under your personal control (and can even be enjoyable as you put into action only those strategies that have been proven successful). That's right. All professional services marketing success boils down to you as an individual. But, don't take our word for it. See how the best business generators operate. The top producers know that what prospects and clients buy is you—your expertise, ability to communicate and capability to solve their problems. Realize that you are the product—and you are also your own product manager and sales force. Take control now of your personal marketing strategy.

Here's a final point to keep in mind before we proceed. *The best business generators know that business development is a skill, just as your legal services are based on your personal skills.* Moreover, as a professional, you already possess a great deal of the personal skills you need to bring in a lot of work. Using the best business generators as a model, all you need to do is to apply your existing strengths—and build a few more skills on a focused, disciplined basis. You don't need to be a natural-born salesperson or self-promoter to excel. You just have to shift your thinking a bit—and practice a consistent, step-by-step system on a daily basis.

HOW DO YOU BECOME MORE LIKE THE BEST BUSINESS GENERATORS?

Think about someone that you know who excels at business development. Consider their personal style. What personal skills are strongest? How do they relate to their clients? How do they spend their time? *What do they do that others at your firm don't do?*

Keep your conclusions in mind as we go on. Compare your impressions to the attributes that we'll be covering here.

As you'll see in this chapter, we've isolated two basic sets of key factors that drive the business development success of the top producers. Let's introduce these two aspects now—and cover them in more detail later in this chapter. Specifically, rainmakers excel due to their *attitudes* and *aptitudes*.

ATTITUDES

This means that the best business generators share a *common mind-set*: they *think* about business development in a way that amplifies the intensity, vitality, and quality of their practice building effort.

> They work harder and smarter at it. They see business development possibilities in all aspects of their workday. And they enjoy the entrepreneurial challenge of building their personal base of business.

Working through this chapter, you'll see how you can build and reinforce these same attitudes. Because, your ATTITUDE is under your PERSONAL CONTROL—you can shift the way you think about your day. By setting the proper goals and reinforcing them on a disciplined, daily basis, you'll begin to think like the top producers do. You'll see how this attitude translates into greater, more productive activity and, ultimately, more new business.

APTITUDES

Even though the top business generators have different personalities and operating styles, they DO share similar business development habits, plans of attack and personal marketing systems.

> Said differently, the best producers emphasize the same step-by-step priorities in their personal plan of attack on a daily basis. And this consistency accounts for their success.

Once you understand WHAT this personal marketing system entails and WHY it leads to success, you can concentrate on HOW to use this step-by-step, systematic approach to build your own practice. Simply put, if you START DOING THE SAME THINGS, THEN YOU'LL START TO PRODUCE SIMILAR RESULTS.

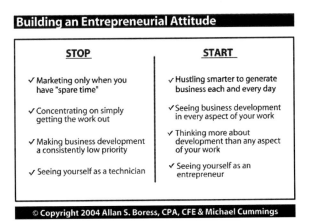

WHY YOUR BUSINESS DEVELOPMENT *ATTITUDE* IS THE FOUNDATION OF YOUR SUCCESS

There is one clear lesson that we've learned over the years:

WE FEEL THAT BUILDING THE RIGHT ATTITUDE IS ABOUT 80% OF YOUR PERSONAL MARKETING SUCCESS.

Let's make this clear. Frankly, without a shift in your thinking, *no amount of "marketing know how" will matter.*

Why? Because, we've proven time and time again that achieving breakthroughs in personal marketing, client development and selling means that you first must change how you think about your business day, your job and your personal strengths. Otherwise, you won't make the changes in your day-to-day action steps that lead to success.

Let's see how the "right" thinking will drive your success:

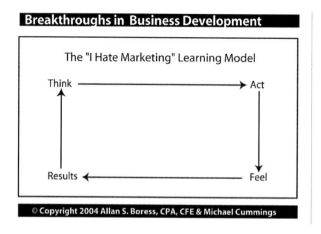

Breakthroughs in Business Development

The "I Hate Marketing" Learning Model

Think ⟶ Act

Results ⟵ Feel

© Copyright 2004 Allan S. Boress, CPA, CFE & Michael Cummings

HERE'S WHAT THIS MEANS FOR YOU:

Basically, the way you THINK about business development determines the way you ACT.

For example, if you see yourself as a technician—then you'll ACT like a technician. That denotes that you'll focus more on getting the work out and dedicate yourself to the high technical quality of your work product. There is nothing wrong with that way of thinking.

If you want to get better at business development, you've got to build a strong business development ATTITUDE (thinking process). That may require a simple shift in the way you think about your daily priorities. For example, the best business generators see the business development aspects in everything they do. They see the delivery of a work product to a client as a "relationship building" opportunity. Therefore, instead of simply mailing out a contract, they ACT differently than others. They take it out to the client, explain the results, discuss the implications, and find other ways to be of service. Without the right attitude, the best business generators wouldn't have taken the kind of ACTION that turns into new business.

The second important point is this. The right thinking makes you set the right DAILY PRIORITIES— SO YOU CONSISTENTLY TAKE THE RIGHT KIND OF ACTIONS. Linking the right attitudes with the right aptitudes—means that you'll aim towards taking the ACTIONS THAT ARE MOST PRODUCTIVE IN BUILDING YOUR PRACTICE. And you'll do it consistently.

Therefore, if you THINK about business development in the right way and take the best ACTIONS consistently and systematically, you'll FEEL better about business development. You'll feel IN CONTROL, as you'll discover that you can get direct results through added effort.

Also, you'll feel more COMFORTABLE and CONFIDENT in your business development capability. And, ultimately, you'll feel more ENTHUSIASTIC about business development—and eager to do more.

Eventually, you'll experience the tangible RESULTS that you're after. The right thinking means that you take consistent actions. Then, your practice will grow with new clients, vital networks, additional business with existing clients and more referrals. And these results will vitalize you even further.

Accordingly, this is the right place to start—thinking about business development in the right way. The best business generators have learned to think in a specific way over time—and so can you.

HOW TO BUILD YOUR BUSINESS DEVELOPMENT ATTITUDE

We've identified *three key attitudes* that distinguish the best business generators from everyone else:

#1: THEY HUSTLE SMARTER.

They get into more business development action on a daily basis than others do. Their success is not based on being "lucky" or "well-connected". Nor is it based on a grand marketing strategy. Instead, they do the basic practice building steps each and every day—no matter what else interferes.

#2: THEY BLEED BUSINESS DEVELOPMENT.

They think MORE about business development than they do about other aspects of their job. Moreover, they SEE BUSINESS DEVELOPMENT POSSIBILITIES IN EVERYTHING THEY DO—whether it's work related or socially.

#3: THEY SEE THEMSELVES AS ENTREPRENEURS

Their mindset is that of entrepreneurs instead of solely as attorneys. They think about ways to grow their business—how to seize new marketing opportunities. They relate with clients, prospects and referrals as fellow "business persons"—rather than as technically driven attorneys.

Stop for a second. Take a look at these attitudes once again. Now, start with the first attitude. How might this differ from an average producer? In fact, what would be the "polar opposite" attitude that one might display?

Repeat this process for the next two attitudes. Again, what would be typical attitude? And, what would be the opposite extreme thinking?

Now, take a look at the exhibit below. See how your answers compare to what we typically find. In the left column, labeled **STOP**—we've identified those attitudes that will inhibit your growth as a business developer. Unfortunately, these attitudes are ingrained in many of the average producers in the profession. Sadly, this attitude will limit their ability to grow their practice.

You want to shift over to the attitudes depicted in the **START** column. This will take a conscious effort and daily reinforcement. And, it *can* be done. And, the results are truly empowering.

Let's see how you can build the first business development attitude—hustling smarter.

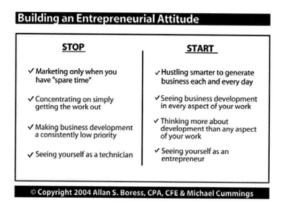

Building an Entrepreneurial Attitude

STOP	START
✓ Marketing only when you have "spare time"	✓ Hustling smarter to generate business each and every day
✓ Concentrating on simply getting the work out	✓ Seeing business development in every aspect of your work
✓ Making business development a consistently low priority	✓ Thinking more about development than any aspect of your work
✓ Seeing yourself as a technician	✓ Seeing yourself as an entrepreneur

© Copyright 2004 Allan S. Boress, CPA, CFE & Michael Cummings

HOW TO "HUSTLE SMARTER"

The first attitude of the best business generators in the legal profession is to HUSTLE SMARTER, which means they get into more business development action on a DAILY basis.

We've found this attitude in each top producer that we've worked with over the years. Perhaps the best example was one of the top producers that Mike met while working at Arthur Andersen & Co. This man had single-handedly transformed a medium-sized office from a meek market presence to the dominant accounting firm in his town over a five year time frame. And this growth was largely due to his personal efforts. In fact, his reputation for being aggressive at business development was so renowned, he was nicknamed the "Great White Shark"—and he was proud of it. Eager to learn his secrets of practice development, Mike asked him about it one day. Here's a direct quote:

> All I do is write down five business development action steps each day on my "To-Do" list. And, no matter what, I make sure that I follow through on these five things. Some days I do more and other opportunities arise without me having to generate them—but I always do those five things.

Now, take five action steps a day. Multiply it by five days a week and you get 25 actions a week. OK, multiply 25 action steps a week by 50 weeks a year, and you get 1,250 actions steps taken in a year at a minimum. I know that my average competitors aren't approaching this amount of activity. So, even if I was a complete moron, I'd get SOME business out of what I'm doing.

I found that the harder I worked at business development, the luckier I got. And, over time, I've gotten smarter. Now, I know which marketing activities pay off—and which are useless.

It's sounds almost too simple. But, it's true. To get results from business development you have to find a way to do more of it on a daily basis. That's what we call hustling smarter. Here are some examples.

- "Hustle" is the difference between THINKING about all the people that you could be contacting—versus contacting two each day.

- "Hustle" is the difference between going to lunch by yourself or with a colleague at your firm—versus taking a client out to lunch and discussing their business, listening to their problems, and looking for more ways to serve them.

- "Hustle" is the difference between simply attending a conference and passively listening to the speakers—versus actively "working the conference" and systematically making good contacts.

Therefore, "hustle" means doing more business development each and every day *by setting minimum acceptable standards* for activity and then following through on a disciplined, daily basis.

Right now, we imagine that a lot of you are complaining. We know—you're already busy. You've got to manage your projects, answer client phone calls, review the work of others and get your own work done. You're swamped. That's the BAD NEWS about hustling smarter.

But the GOOD NEWS is that it's not that difficult to out-hustle the vast majority of your competitors. Because they use the fact that they are busy to put off doing anything at all.

What we found is that *hustle is really a mindset.* And it's a conscious decision that you have to make each and every day. That's right. It's not necessarily working longer hours. It's just doing a few things each and every day. You build marketing actions into your schedule and squeeze the most you can out of them.

So, what are some ways that you can hustle smarter? Here is what can do:

1. START SMALL.

Aim to do just one or two more business development actions each day for the next month. It doesn't have to be anything major. Keep it simple. For example, clip an article and have your assistant mail it to a client, prospect or referral source with a personal note attached. Or make a phone call and invite a client to lunch next week. WHAT you do is LESS IMPORTANT right now.

We're after getting you to make it a DAILY HABIT.

And, over time, to build in more and more action as you see fit.

Even by itself, this approach can have a big payoff for you. Here's an example: Recently, after attending one of our training programs, a young staff person realized he had to do more business development to progress in his career. He decided his ONE business development action would be to ask his favorite client for a referral.

Realize that this took a bit of courage, since he had never done it before. So, he scheduled the lunch and asked for the referral. Guess what happened? He got one! More so, it turned into a sizeable client for his firm.

Now, reflect back on this example. Hustling smarter really boiled down to a making a simple decision. And taking control by scheduling a lunch with that particular client.

Now, what are some other ways that you can HUSTLE SMARTER?

2. MAKE SURE THAT YOU USE YOUR LUNCHES AND BREAKFASTS TO MARKET AND SELL._

Let's face it. You have to eat anyway—even when you are super busy. So, use this time more effectively to make contact with people who can help you. It can be a client, attorney, banker or somebody else who can bring you work.

BUT, don't just go to lunch and talk about anything. You must have a pre-defined business development purpose in mind. You want to be in control. For example, let's say that you're having lunch with a banker. What's your goal? You want to explore what mutual opportunities exist and how you can promote together. Find out if she has any customers who are dissatisfied with their representation and secure an introduction.

In other words, we suggest that you have an AGENDA for lunch. Go to meetings with a purpose. Find specific ways to do more business.

Make lunches and breakfasts your "sacred" marketing time. Schedule them out in advance. You'll find yourself "hustling smarter" more quickly and quite painlessly by using this tactic.

Here's another idea:

3. SET "GIVE-UP" GOALS.

This means that if you're going to add more business development actions into your daily routine—then you have to FREE UP time by eliminating other activities. Otherwise, you won't get to follow through on the NEW business development priorities.

In other words, if you are going to do MORE business development—you'll have to do LESS of something else.

Here's an example of what we mean. We had a client who found that she was going to a lot of technical conferences—where there was little or no business development possibility.

After thinking about it, she decided to cancel her registration at a technical conference—even though she enjoyed it. Instead, she went to a conference that was organized by an industry association that was recommended by one of her clients. When she arrived, she found there were lots of prospective clients that she could mingle with. As a result, she met a prospect who became a very important client.

So, she "gave up" a time consuming activity with NO business development possibility—in return for an activity with a solid business development purpose.

Stop here for just a second. Think about how your day is set up. Take a look at your calendar for today. Could you have substituted a business development action for something on your "to-do" list? Look for the items that you can eliminate or delegate to someone else and replace them with business development action.

Also, consider a business development action that you could get others to do on your behalf. Could your assistant or staff get some letters out for you? What else could they do that would free up your time?

Here's a final suggestion on how to hustle smarter that you can start thinking about:

4. FILL YOUR "DOWN TIME" WITH BUSINESS DEVELOPMENT ACTIVITY.

Even if you're a good time manager, you still face some down time. Consider how can you fill it up with business development action.

For example, if you take a train to work, don't read the newspaper on the way. Write personal notes to clients and prospects instead. Review your schedule to brainstorm on what you can do to bring in business today.

Or, you're in a reception area—waiting to meet with your client. Don't just sit around. Make a few phone calls instead—while you have the chance. Or jot down the referrals or introductions that you want to request from this client. Perhaps, grab the industry journal sitting on the credenza. Spot an article that applies to one of your service areas. Make it a point to mention it to your client.

Or, when you're in your car. Don't just listen to your car radio—listen to a tape on business development instead. Get audiotapes of important industry conferences so that you are up to speed. Use the car phone to keep in touch.

Now, take a look back at these 4 ideas. We recognize that you're busy—you're not like a salesperson who is supposed to be selling all of the time. But, consider the best business generators. Don't you think that they're busy too? In fact, many of them are in leadership positions at their firm and this puts even more demands on their time. Nevertheless, despite these scheduling burdens, they MAKE the time to hustle.

So, all we ask you to do is to try the same approach. CONSCIOUSLY squeeze more business development into your day. Fill in the gaps in your schedule with solid business development. That's what we're talking about when we suggest that you hustle SMARTER.

To help you get started, we've put together the following personal brainstorming exercise. Take some time out right now to complete it.

HUSTLING SMARTER: PERSONAL BRAINSTORMING EXERCISE #1

Start to put these ideas to work for you.

Remember, the key to hustling smarter is to make business development a consistently top priority in your daily schedule.

Take a moment. Get out your daily calendar, as well as a note pad to jot down some ideas. Look at your schedule for the next week or two.

STEP #1: ADD ONE MORE BUSINESS DEVELOPMENT ACTION EACH DAY.

Set a goal to add at least 10–12 business development actions for the upcoming two weeks.

Consider all of your possibilities.

- Clip an article and send it to a few clients.

- Call a referral source to get re-acquainted.

- Join a new association.

- Meet with a colleague.

If you're having trouble coming up with ideas, go ask a top producer in your firm for some advice. Also, are there any business development actions you've been procrastinating on? Commit to getting to them this week.

STEP #2: USE YOUR BREAKFASTS AND LUNCHES TO MARKET AND SELL.

Take a look at your schedule for breakfasts and lunches. How many of these have business development possibilities? What do you have to do in order to turn this into a marketing or selling opportunity?

Do you have any open slots? Make it a point to fill them up with business development. Invite a client, referral source, partner or colleague to join you.

STEP #3: SET "GIVE UP" GOALS.

We added some actions in steps 1 and 2. Now, let's subtract some. Look at your schedule and review your to-do lists. What actions can you delegate to others to free up business development time? Can you eliminate any activities outright? Are there any additional business development activities that you can leverage off to a junior professional or an administrative person?

STEP #4: GO THE EXTRA MILE.

· Look at what you've accomplished thus far. This is how the best business generators manage their calendar and set priorities. How much additional action did you come up with?

Now, look at your "to-do" list from a different perspective. Imagine that you didn't draw a salary at all. Instead, let's say that your full income was derived from the additional work that you sold to clients, as well as from the fees generated from new clients that you brought in.

With this fresh mindset, review your calendar once again. How much more business development could you fit in? Would you add a few more business development breakfasts/lunches? Could you find other activities to delegate?

The purpose of this last step is to get you even more closely "tuned" into the best business generators' frame of mind. After all, the best business generators sell and market AS IF their professional livelihood depended on it!

If you're a sole practitioner or managing partner, you may already have this orientation. Others of you will have to strengthen your resolve—and set more aggressive daily activity goals. In other words, sell and market AS IF your professional success depends on your ability to bring in business. ACT "AS IF" you were on full commission, instead of salary. Then, bring this frame of mind to your daily setting of priorities. You'll find that the harder and smarter you work at business development —the luckier you'll get.

HOW TO BLEED BUSINESS DEVELOPMENT

The next key attitude is BLEEDING BUSINESS DEVELOPMENT.

The best business generators see business development possibilities in EVERY aspect of their day. Whether they are meeting with clients, calling a client's banker, attending a chamber of commerce lunch, or planning their social calendar—somehow and someway they'll find a business development "tie-in".

Rainmakers see business development possibilities in even the most routine and mundane activities. Take billing, for example. Many top producers don't simply send an impersonal bill out to their clients. They may send along a brief memo that summarizes the VALUE of the work to the client— instead of simply the cost associated. Some break out all of the individual parts of what they do on the billing, for instance all of the individual steps of the engagement so the client can see the real value, other than a cold number of dollars due.

For important clients or those they haven't seen for a while, they may walk it over. And they sell the client on the value they're producing.

Their "antennae for new business" is always up. They look at every situation—a lunch, a golf outing or even a wedding as an opportunity. They are in the habit of thinking about generating business —it's in their consciousness.

Here's an illustration. This is a true story of one of our clients. The daughter of the managing partner was getting married. At the wedding reception, the managing partner was standing in the receiving line and saw somebody that he'd never met before. He introduced himself and quickly discovered that this person owned his own manufacturing business. The managing partner made a mental note to seek out this person later. After dinner, as he circulated around the room, he found this guest and engaged him in a very short conversation about him and his business. Wouldn't you know it? The guest wasn't pleased with the current firm advising him on his succession plan. The managing partner told us he said the following words to his guest: "I'm the managing partner of the XYZ law firm. Should we be talking about your business?" That was his "close."

The result? By listening—by keeping his business development antenna up—he caught a prospective client in the "buying cycle" and created the appointment that turned into a new client, right at his daughter's wedding.

So, the best business generators simply think about business development MORE OFTEN, because they see it as the most important part of their job and their career. So, when they plan out their day, they are constantly thinking about how business development can be factored in; it's always their top priority.

So, now let's look at how you can begin to bleed business development:

1. FIRST, THINK ABOUT WHAT YOU LIKE TO DO THAT CAN SERVE A BUSINESS DEVELOPMENT PURPOSE.

The best of all worlds is if you enjoy something AND it brings you lots of business. It's also easier to DO MORE of activities that you like.

Start finding ways to do more of those activities right now. Get the most business development payback possible. For example, if you enjoy networking, make sure that you are in the right organizations. Find the associations with the highest concentration of clients and prospects.

Or, if you like writing articles, contact the editor of a newsletter or magazine that caters to the type of clients that you want to attract. Pinpoint an area of interest or a common problem that their readers face. After you write the article, make sure that you use it to create business by mailing copies to all of your targets and clients.

Perhaps, you like to speak at seminars. Find an opportunity to speak where clients and prospects gather. Load your presentation up with references to your client experiences. Be sure to get a list of attendees and follow up with a personal note.

Don't stop here. What social and community actions do you enjoy? Are you into golf? Find clients, prospects and referral sources with a similar passion. Join the golf and country clubs where you can find prospective clients. Become visible in activities that showcase your business expertise. It doesn't have to be golf. Are you active in your church? Do you enjoy charitable work? Little league? Boy or Girl Scouts?

It almost doesn't matter which activity you choose initially. Just find a way to factor in business development. The marketing rule to remember is: *"Wherever you go, you'll find business"*

2. WORK WITH THE TOP PRODUCERS AT YOUR FIRM

Find a way to learn from the top producers at your firm. See if they'd be willing to coach you a bit—or mentor you. Why shouldn't they? It's in their best interest to have you bring in more business; it's going to fall into their pocket.

How should you work together? Initially, meet with them. Find out what their plans are to build their practice over the next year. Find out what problems and obstacles have kept them from selling more business. See how you might help to solve some of these problems. For instance, they may need help in following through on the large number of leads that they already have. Or, they may see opportunities that they don't have time to pursue. Perhaps they have referral sources that they can't stay in touch with consistently.

Here's an example of this process.

A partner at one of our clients wanted help from one of the big producers at his firm—who resided in Washington. So, he had to figure out a way for this rainmaker to come to New York to help him build his local practice. He was stumped. What could he offer this person who was the best business generator in the entire firm? Well, he figured that he had nothing to lose. So, he called the partner in Washington and asked him. How could they help each other out? To his surprise, he found that the Washington partner lacked the resources and time needed to complete a pet project. So, they made a deal. The New York partner would contribute some staff resources and supervise the project to completion. In return, the rainmaker would guide and counsel him. And, more importantly, he'd introduce the partner from New York to his existing Washington based clients who had strong New York connections.

In our experience, this story is not uncommon. How can you leverage off the success of a top producer at your firm? How can you work together in a way that's mutually beneficial?

3. WORK WITH TOP PRODUCER AT ALLIED FIRMS

Now, go beyond the top producers at your firm. Think about the attorneys, bankers, insurance agents and others that you work with closely. Which ones excel at business development? Do you have good personal chemistry with this person? Do you feel comfortable?

Take the next step. Set up a lunch meeting. Tap into their brain. How did they build their practices? What seems to work best for them? Do they see mutual advantage in marketing together with you?

If nothing else, schedule lunch meetings periodically, just to share ideas. You'll find that the top producers have turned business development into a game, like golf. And they similarly love to share new ideas about how to get better at this "game," just as they would for other pursuits. Better yet, find a way to work together more closely.

Here's an example. One attorney that we know came up with a novel approach.

He specialized in estate and business planning for family owned companies. In this work, he had teamed up with a respected insurance agent. And, on occasion, he worked with an attorney and a consulting psychologist that specialized in family business issues. Most of them were pretty good business generators in their own right, but the insurance agent was a superb marketer. He agreed to mentor the others.

They decided to organize monthly business development meetings. They'd review each other's promotional materials and discuss enhancements. Over time, they identified opportunities for joint marketing. They began to invite guest speakers to brainstorm on additional ways to bring in business.

Needless to say, they ended up trading some pretty heavy business back and forth. But, more importantly, they became a "support group." They helped each other to foster a consistent business development effort, *and they all benefited.*

4. ENHANCE YOUR BUSINESS DEVELOPMENT SKILLS.

The fourth way to bleed business development is to become more skillful and adept at it. Let's face it: if you think you're inadequate at something, you won't like it. And you certainly won't seek out opportunities to do more of it.

However, if something is truly important to you, then you'll look for any technique, approach or tool that might help you to perform better.

In our business, we often conduct in-house personal marketing and professional sales training workshops for law firms. Guess who sits in the front row paying full attention? Who do you think takes the most copious notes? Which ones participate most in the training and attempt to apply the techniques when they leave?

You guessed it. It's the best business generators—the people who already excel at business development. They are the most enthusiastic students.

Here's an example, we were conducting a training session for a law firm in St.. Louis.

In the morning session, we covered listening and interviewing techniques that make you more productive in face-to-face selling. About 20 minutes before the lunch break, the managing partner excused himself. He explained that he had a long-standing lunch appointment with a prospective client. But, before the training, he had planned to "make a presentation." After hearing what we had to say in the morning, he decided to leave his presentation at the office. Instead, he would simply listen and interview the prospect—using the techniques he had just learned.

After lunch, he returned to the class. It turns out that he made the sale. But, more importantly, he sold the prospect a DIFFERENT SERVICE than the one he would have presented to him. In other words, he would have tried to sell the prospect something that the prospect didn't want to buy.

He made a sale he might have missed if he wasn't open to hearing new ideas or learning new skills.

Take a cue from the best business generators. Work on your business development skills. What skills do you need to get better at?

Here are a few to consider:

- Public speaking;

- Persuasive writing;

- Personal marketing;

- Professional selling skills;

- Relationship management;

- Designing presentations;

- Networking skills;

- Working industry conferences;

- Special services

- Various certification courses

Before you go on, ask yourself a question. What skills are going to be most important for your success? Isn't business development at the top of the list? Now, pick a course. Get signed up today.

Believe us. Business development is a learnable skill—it's not solely a natural talent. Anybody can improve and excel over time. But, you have to want it and work at it—just like you've worked hard to build your technical skills.

And remember, the more skillful you become the more you'll like business development. Consequently, you'll be spurred on to do even more.

Let's move on now to the final way to BLEED BUSINESS DEVELOPMENT.

5. RECOGNIZE THAT YOU'RE ALREADY MARKETING & SELLING ALL THE TIME

We briefly talked about this earlier. You're already marketing and selling all the time—even if you don't realize it. When you do work for your clients, you are always sending a marketing message. Every interaction with a client indicates how much you care about them and how well you understand their business. Based on your "marketing", they may perceive you as a valued advisor—or, instead, they could view you as simply a technician. Your success in "marketing" your quality of work and service determines whether your clients continue to hire you—and whether to ask you for more help.

When you go to lunch with a prospective client or a referral source—you are making some kind of "marketing" impression. If you handle the event properly, they'll see you as a valued contact. One that impresses them enough to refer clients to for service. However, if you don't "market" right, the referrals will never come.

You are also "selling ideas" all the time. Whether you trying to persuade a client to write off their inventory or to get their financial records to you on a timely basis—it's ALL SELLING.

Remember,
YOU ARE THE MARKETING MESSAGE.

So, what do you do? Treat all-important interactions as a "marketing opportunity". That's what the best business generators do.

When you go to lunch with a client, don't think about what you want to eat. Instead, think about your interviewing strategy. You want to find out what your client's aches, hurts, needs wants, concerns and desires are. What are the key problems they're facing? What can you do to enhance the quality of your client relationship? What ideas do you have to improve this client's business?

Likewise, if you are networking at an association meeting, you are sending out a personal marketing message with everyone you meet. How do you introduce yourself? What questions do you ask? Do you try to meet people?

---

*Always go to a marketing event with
an agenda. Go with a specific business
development purpose.*

We've now covered five specific ways that you can begin to bleed business development. Take some time out right now. Work through the following brainstorming exercises to tailor these ideas for your practice.

BLEED BUSINESS DEVELOPMENT: PERSONAL BRAINSTORMING EXERCISE #2

The predominant reason that the top producers sell a lot of work is that they see business development in all aspects of their job. They enjoy it. They think about it constantly. And they are always seeking out the opportunity to help their clients and prospects to solve their business problems.

Now, take out a fresh piece of paper. Set aside a few minutes of quiet time to brainstorm.

STEP #1: DO THE THINGS YOU LIKE TO DO THAT CAN RESULT IN MORE BUSINESS.

Remember that the best way to enjoy business development is to concentrate on those activities that you enjoy—the ones that interest you and where you feel comfortable and confident.

Think about your personal interests—whether it's community activities, business associations, sports, etc. Consider ways that you can turn these activities into a fertile business development purpose.

> For example, if you enjoy tennis, ask a client to join you for a set or two. If you are in a business association, consider how you can get into a visible role in order to meet prospective clients.

Next, consider those business development activities that you enjoy. Do you like spending time with the top executives at your clients? Do you enjoy networking or do you prefer writing articles? Do you prefer writing personal notes or calling people up on the phone? Do you enjoy public speaking or putting on seminars?

STEP #2: WORK WITH THE TOP PRODUCERS AT YOUR FIRM.

Which partners bring in a lot of business at your firm? Which of these people do you have the best rapport and personal chemistry? Would they be willing to mentor you? Set up a meeting and ask this person to advise you on the best immediate ways to build your personal practice.

STEP #3: WORK WITH THE TOP PRODUCERS AT ALLIED FIRMS.

Do you know an attorney, banker or other contact that excels at building their practice? Consider perhaps someone who may act as an adviser to one of your clients? Again, do you have solid personal chemistry with this contact? Make a point to take them to lunch. Ask them how they've built their practice. What are their plans for perpetuating this growth? What advice do they have for you?

STEP #4: WORK ON YOUR BUSINESS DEVELOPMENT SKILLS.

Consider how you can enhance your personal marketing and selling skills. What skills are going to be most important in your success? Would you like to be a better public speaker? Do you need to strengthen a special expertise through additional training? Would you like to improve your skills in face-to-face selling?

Find out what training courses that others recommend. Commit to taking a training course in marketing or selling over the next three weeks.

STEP #5: RECOGNIZE THAT YOU'RE ALREADY MARKETING AND SELLING ALL OF THE TIME.

Do you have a meeting coming up with a client? How can you structure the agenda so that you can turn this into a marketing opportunity? How can you help this client further? What can you do to improve your relationship with this individual?

HOW DO HUSTLING SMARTER AND BLEEDING BUSINESS DEVELOPMENT COMPLEMENT EACH OTHER?

TIME OUT! Think back. Can you see how the first two attitudes of the best business generators play off one another? If you bleed business development, that is, if you think about it more often and you learn to like it, naturally, you're going to want to do more business development on a daily basis—consequently you'll hustle smarter.

All that really is required is a decision: to make a simple shift in your thinking. See that business development enters all aspects of your day. Although you may not look at it this way currently, you are marketing and selling ALL of the time.

Let's move on to the final attitude.

HOW TO ACT LIKE AN ENTREPRENEUR

The best business generators see themselves as entrepreneurs rather than solely as attorneys. This means that they believe their PRIMARY PURPOSE is building their practice. Because of this, marketing, selling, client relationship management, quality service and cross marketing is ALWAYS top of mind.

Even early in their careers, they understood that in order to move ahead, they had to take responsibility for building their own book of business; they couldn't wait around for someone to hand feed them work for the rest of their careers and still expect to progress.

They knew that they were in business for themselves.

This DOESN'T mean that they don't value their technical qualifications. It simply means that they LEVERAGE on others to supplement and play this role.

This attitude has an important business development implication. As entrepreneurs, the top producers tend to have a broader business perspective instead of a strict legal perspective. Said differently, they tend to see business issues as a business owner might view them. Consequently, the best business generators are MORE LIKE THEIR CLIENTS. *As a result, clients relate much better to them—not as technicians but as fellow businesspersons.*

Again, don't take our word for it. Listen to your clients.

In our market research work with professional service firms, what clients continually tell us is that they wish that their service provider would get off of the technical details. Instead, they want to hear the business implications. What are the critical problems you see? What solutions do you suggest? What action should your client take? That's where the best business generators excel. They are able to persuade the prospect to engage them because they speak directly to the needs, values and concerns of the client and prospect. Put another way, THEY SPEAK THEIR CLIENT'S LANGUAGE—using their words and vocabulary.

You don't have to believe us. Numerous studies have been conducted with CEO's to ascertain how they selected the winning law firm. Universally, the conclusions are the same. But, here are some findings that were published in a study by one of the state bar associations: When they ranked the most important reasons they selected their law firm, the winning difference the decision-makers identified were (10 is the highest rank):

Concern for helping the company make more money	9.2
Rapport; close interpersonal working relationship between the contact partner and the company's key executives	8.8
Ability and willingness to listen and help identify, understand and resolve the company's business problems	8.5
Exhibiting a proactive attitude; anticipating problems and, especially, opportunities	7.5
Timeliness of performing services	7.3
Periodic, regular non-engagement contact	7.0
Responsiveness to client service request	7.0

(For comparison sake, technical expertise is rated 3.5 and fees are 5.8.)

DO YOU SEE WHAT YOUR CLIENTS AND PROSPECTS ARE TELLING YOU?

Let's sum up. The best business generators see themselves as entrepreneurs. And this entrepreneurial viewpoint allows them to "tune-into" the wavelength of their clients. In turn, this enhances their position as a business advisor and strengthens the rapport they have with business owners.

So, how can you act more like an entrepreneur?

1. SPECIALIZE IN A FEW INDUSTRIES:

We'll talk about this in detail in a later chapter. More and more, our clients are specializing in a handful of industries. Let's face it. You can't be all things to all people. So, make the tough choice to become immersed in two or three industries.

Why does this make sense? Why should you build your industry know-how? Because that's what your clients care about. That's what they'll respect. That's what they'll say about you to their peers.

This is why industry specialization is the cornerstone of the marketing strategy for the vast majority of law firms. And most of the top producers specialize in a few industries. They focus. They know that this strengthens their appeal to clients and prospects.

Here's an example.

When Mike worked at Arthur Andersen & Co., the industry program was instrumental in marketing the firm's services. Consequently, Mike worked closely with the partners in charge of the industry specialties like manufacturing, health care, banking, real estate, construction, government and others.

One of the industry partners that he worked with had an interesting perspective on the importance of industry specialization. He made the following observation:

"It's funny. These industry partners are some of the best marketers in the firm. In fact, they are so tuned into the industries they specialize in that they NOW look, act and sound JUST LIKE THEIR CLIENTS. The government partner is a suave politician. The manufacturing guys are gruff since they spend so much on the shop floor, and the banking partners are more conservative, reserved, and sedately dressed . . . just like bankers.

"Think about the real estate specialists. What do they look like? How do they speak? How do they dress? These guys are all dressed in flashy European suits with expensive watches and gold chains. They are always talking about deal-making, not abstract contract law.

"The funny part is that when we graduated from college and joined the firm 20 years ago we were all pretty similar in manner and dress. But, as we specialized, we all became different."

Although this particular story relates to a now defunct accounting firm, it has strong implications for all attorneys who seek to develop their practices. Therefore, the first step in acting like an entrepreneur is to choose the specialties that you'll focus on.

2. LISTEN TO YOUR CLIENTS AND IDENTIFY THEIR CONCERNS:

How much do you know about your top client's business? Are you up on the concerns that are driving their industry? What's most important to your clients?

The best way to position yourself as an entrepreneur in the eyes of your clients is to ASK THEM QUESTIONS AND LISTEN.

Learn their priorities, as that is what's important to them. And that's why they need you. Ask them questions that go beyond their legal perspectives. Find out what challenges they face in operations, service and management systems.

This sounds simple, but it works. Too few attorneys engage their clients (and prospective clients) in conversations like these.

3. IMMERSE YOURSELF IN AN INDUSTRY:

Even if you specialize in several industries, we suggest that you pick one or two as your "super specialties". Then, blitz these areas and deepen your understanding of this industry.

What's the best way to do this? Enlist the aid of your top clients who are in this industry. What are the best associations? Which one would be best for meeting top executives at prospect companies? What newsletters and magazines do these clients read to stay on top of the industry? What is the best way to market yourself and network in this industry?

Here are some other ideas.

Walk trade shows with these clients. This is a good way to get introduced to companies just like your clients', and their suppliers. If there are educational sessions going on at the show sit next to your client at the presentations and see how the topic impacts your client's business.

Meet with the leaders of the local industry association. Talk to the president, membership chairman, and head of the program committee. Get their perspective on the top business concerns that their members face. Which of the members is particularly knowledgeable? Can you get an introduction to this person?

Also, interview the editors of the top newsletters and magazines that serve this industry. What's their editorial focus? Why? What are their reader's concerns?

Make it a project to learn all you can about this industry. Get some help from your staff or administrative people. Start an industry information file. Get them to read selected industry periodicals and highlight the relevant articles. Or, have them go to a library. Xerox the table of contents from back issues of the industry periodicals. Then, get copies of the articles that look best.

Some partners tell us they couldn't get their staff to pursue industry knowledge, especially on their own time. Why shouldn't they? Where does it say that they don't have to help you build your practice? How can they expect continual increases in pay and opportunities for advancement, unless they do their fair share of increasing their productivity and value to the client and prospective clients?

Consider a special research study—perhaps in concert with an association or industry periodical. Conduct a study that identifies the critical business concerns facing the industry. Convene a special focus group where clients and prospects share their business concerns, current priorities and future plans.

Or, collect financial and operating benchmarking information. Calculate key industry ratios. Compare these ratios to some of your client results.

Here's another idea. Hire an industry "guru" to speak to a small group of your clients. Get them to invite some colleagues along. Alternatively, rent a videotape by the expert or link into a teleconference and take the same approach.

Now, once you immerse yourself in an industry, gear the bulk of your marketing to this industry. Being an entrepreneur means that you can see the world through the eyes of your clients. You see their needs and find a way to help them. You should strive to know what your clients care about. And your marketing results will multiply.

If you look back on these ideas, you may already be doing some of them. These principles are tried and true methods.

The point here is INTENSITY. What we suggest is an all out blitz on an industry—a full court press. Put almost ALL your energy into an industry.

A QUICK SUMMARY OF THE ATTITUDES OF THE BEST BUSINESS GENERATORS

Lets' take a look at what you accomplished so far. You now know the three critical attitudes that the top business generators possess.

So to improve your business development results, you need to ask yourself a basic question:

HOW CAN I BUILD THESE SAME BUSINESS DEVELOPMENT ATTITUDES?

Really, all you have to do is to shift your thinking. Find a way to HUSTLE SMARTER—that is to get into more action on a daily basis. Start BLEEDING BUSINESS DEVELOPMENT. Think MORE about business development—and LESS about your other on your day-to-day distractions. And, finally, ACT LIKE AN ENTREPRENEUR—get in tune with your client's point of view. Understand their industry issues, business concerns and personal goals.

All it takes is a decision. Decide to think about business development like the best business generators do. That's a decision that you can make today.

This, however, is only one-half of the equation. Once you get the THINKING right—you then have to take the right ACTIONS.

Let's move on now and learn about the best business generators' APTITUDES (WHAT ACTIONS THEY TAKE TO BUILD THEIR PRACTICES).

THE PERSONAL MARKETING SYSTEM OF THE BEST BUSINESS GENERATORS

Here's what we're going to cover next. As we said earlier, although the best business generators differ greatly in terms of operating style and personality, they ALL share similar day-to-day business building habits. In other words, they ALL use the same systematic plan of attack . . . and it's an approach that you can begin to emulate.

This personal marketing system defines the specific, custom-tailored, and step-by-step consistent actions that you'll take to achieve superior results. In a sense, this will become your daily personal marketing "TO DO" list. It will build the hustle, consistency and disciplined effort required for mastering business development. Over time, you'll see improvements and successes that will drive you to increased daily marketing action.

OVERVIEW

Here's how you'll build your personal marketing plan through this course. Our goal is to give you a blueprint for building your practice. Again, using the best business generators as a "model of success," you'll build a highly patterned, systematic and disciplined plan of attack.

Here's an outline of the personal marketing system:

- *Step #1: Focus on Your Best Opportunities*

- *Step #2: Market to Your Existing Clients*

- *Step #3: Turn Your Clients into Your Sales Force*

- *Step #4: Build Alliances*

- *Step #5: Develop Your Network*

- *Step #6: Build Your Personal Reputation*

This is how the best business generators build their practice. As you'll see, they put the most important and productive actions first. Here's another critical point, the bulk of the marketing system—steps two through five—all involve relationship marketing. That's the secret of the best business generators' success: *leverage*. By building exceptional relationships, they magnify and amplify their personal marketing effort—and turn others into a sales force for them.

Also, notice that it is an "outside-in" approach. Clients are always your first priority. Then, you build your network. As a final step, you go directly to the outside market.

Now, we'll cover each of these steps in much more detail in the upcoming chapters but, we want to give you a flavor of what we'll be covering. So, just review each of the steps. We'll go into much more detail later.

STEP #1: FOCUS ON YOUR BEST OPPORTUNITIES

The best business generators know that focus is right place to start. Since they are busy, they only go where you they have the best chances for success. These are their golden opportunities.

Where are your golden opportunities? How can you make the most of your strengths and advantages? How can you harness the most out of your service experiences and business know-how? What market niches are best for you? These are all questions that you must answer to best define your focus.

We'll show you how to accomplish this in an upcoming chapter. Basically, you'll think about your top clients. The 20% of your base that accounts for 80% of your revenue. Then, to pick your target niches, you'll "clone" your top clients. In other words, you'll seek to find more clients EXACTLY like your top clients.

So, focus means that YOU DECIDE whom you want to have as clients AND where your market strengths are greatest.

What happens if you don't do this? What do you get if you market generically? You'll end up with a diffuse and weak marketing program. One that looks and sounds like everybody else. You'll cheapen the value of your unique client base, experiences and special skills.

STEP #2: MARKET TO YOUR EXISTING CLIENTS

This is always the first priority for the best business generators. The best business generators know that they are going to get about 50% of their new business from their clients and their referrals. New business is new business, whether it be new services sold to existing clients, repeat business, or referrals to new clients.

The best business generators realize that marketing and selling are a lot like courtship. And the relationship with your clients is a lot like marriage. Like the best business generators, you should never let the romance die in your client relationships. How can you get closer to your clients? How can you stay on top of their critical personal and business concerns?

Moreover, the best business generators recognize that it takes a lot of time and effort to fortify their relationships with their clients. They have to guard against the complacency that can creep into the relationships with their clients. Laziness ultimately may cost them their clients.

Think about it. What is the leading cause of "divorce by your clients?" Is it fees or projects running over budgets? Or is that a symptom of what leads to the divorce? No! We find that more clients are lost due to poor communication and inattention than for any other reason, just like with marriages and other relationships.

Keep this is mind. Your best client is your competitor's best prospective client.

Believe us–*YOUR* clients are being ACTIVELY courted. Losing one of your top clients is really painful and will be difficult, expensive and time consuming to replace.

> See CHAPTER 6: THE ART OF MARKETING TO YOUR EXISTING CLIENTS for in depth strategies on this particular "rule".

STEP #3: TURN YOUR CLIENTS INTO YOUR SALES FORCE

The best business generators know that a referral from a satisfied client is the most important marketing asset at your disposal. Activating this powerful word of mouth advertising by your clients should be a top priority.

Wouldn't it be great if your clients sold for you? That's precisely how most rainmakers built their book of business.

They don't have the time to be constantly marketing themselves. So, what they've done is to build strong relationships with their clients and their clients spread the word for them. This means that they are "PRE-SOLD" into new situations BY THEIR CLIENTS.

This is quite different from a typical attorney. The average producer WAITS for referrals to show up. Instead, the best business generators go out and MAKE REFERRALS HAPPEN.

Think about it? Are you satisfied with the number of referrals that you've received over the last year? How many more could you have gotten just by talking it over with your client? Don't be shy. People like helping other people! So, chances are that your top clients will help you out.

Besides, your clients are likely to understand the value of referrals. Chances are, that's how YOUR clients built THEIR business. Ask them for the same kind of help.

The marketing rule that applies is "Ask and you shall receive." Tap into the great referral networks that your clients possess.

Take heart. It isn't easy to ask for your first referrals. It sounds pushy. But, once you become comfortable with the process, and start doing it time and time again, it will become easy for both parties.

Yes, eventually, you'll have clients calling you—since they'll see referrals as a normal part of your working relationships.

Here's an easy referral to get. Invite a client to lunch and ask them to bring along another executive who might be able to use your services. One of our clients set up a meeting like this recently, expecting one or two potential clients to show up at this gathering. *Instead, 17 new contacts showed up.* He didn't even have to sell himself—since his main client spent 45 minutes singing the praises of this attorney.

How did the client feel about introducing the attorney to his colleagues at the company? Did he feel good about helping them to address their service needs?

Leveraging yourself through your clients' efforts is an easy way to build your practice—if you only do it.

STEP #4A: BUILD INSIDE ALLIANCES

Getting allies in building your practice is critical to leveraging your individual efforts. We'll show you how to build a small number of highly committed and vigorous allies who scout out opportunities for you.

This doesn't always have to be an OUTSIDE ALLY. In fact, the best source of new business and referrals may be the partner, manager or staff person right down the hall.

But, wait. We find that cross marketing rarely happens easily because many partners may "guard" their client relationships—since they worry about potential damage.

So, you have to "sell" others within your firm to send you referrals. Just as with client referrals, you CAN'T SIMPLY ASSUME that referrals are going to come your way.

As we said earlier, the best business generators recognize that cross marketing is essential to building their practice. They want to guarantee that all business from a client stays "IN-HOUSE" and is never taken outside to another firm. Outsiders pose a hazard to the relationship.

Therefore, they take control of the inside game. ***Here are a few strategies they use.***

- *Decide who are your best inside allies:* Find somebody that can be an asset to you. Then consider if you have good personal chemistry with this person. Cross marketing can be risky, so trust is important. Work with someone with common interests and similar goals for building their practice.

- *Make it easy for others to sell your services:* Summarize "danger signals" for your colleagues to keep an eye out for among their clients. Teach them how to qualify their clients' need for your service. Trade short questionnaires that illustrate how to interview clients to determine their need for your service specialty.

- *Nurture the business building possibilities of your project team:* Coach your work team on their role in spotting additional service needs. In many cases, the work team may be closer to some client executives than you are. Have them keep an eye out for the challenges and problems that your client is facing. Work on questions that they should be asking their client counterparts that would signal a service need.

In other words, turn your own people into your sales force as well. Always remember that staff shouldn't simply get the work out. Instead, they must be your eyes and ears at the client—when you're not there. Use a part of your regular client service team meetings to discuss clients' service needs along with your other project issues.

STEP #4B: BUILD OUTSIDE ALLIANCES

Outside your firm, your goal is to aim for a few alliances. That's right—don't look to have ten contacts who each give you a sporadic referral or two. Instead, forge a close working relationship with one or two of the best referral sources and trade a lot of work back and forth.

Be selective about your referral sources. Aim for a select few that you can go to market with—again and again. For an alliance to thrive, it has to work for your mutual benefit. You must get something out of it—and so must your ally.

To make a true alliance work, treat your best referral sources just like your top clients. Make of list of your top three referral sources. Everyday, think about what you can do to improve this relationship and increase business for both of you.

Use the same approach with your external alliances that you use with allies within your own firm. Also look to develop a mutual marketing plan.

Don't worry about how to do this right now. You'll see in our chapter on building alliances where we'll cover the characteristics of effective alliance marketing programs in full detail.

STEP #5: DEVELOP YOUR NETWORK

The experience of the best business generators shows that your reputation is built predominantly through word of mouth advertising, personal referrals and introductions. If you excel at networking, then you ensure a steady stream of market possibilities for your practice. So, we'll show you how to select, join and work the right associations for maximum exposure. Also, you'll devise a personal networking strategy to continually improve and strengthen your contact base.

STEP #6: BUILD YOUR PERSONAL REPUTATION

Take a quick look back at the first five steps. What do these steps have in common?

If you examine them closely, you'll see that all the steps previous to this one are "relationship marketing". This means that you create marketing leverage by building a committed team of people—clients, allies and colleagues at your firm—looking for business to send your way. It also stimulates your most important marketing asset—word of mouth advertising.

This is why you should put 80% of your effort on the first 5 steps. Successful relationship marketing brings you multiples of new business—on a long-term basis.

You still have to go beyond relationship marketing. So, the final step in your marketing system is directly promoting your services to prospective clients.

Don't make the mistake that so many professionals do. When thinking about growing your practice, don't over emphasize this step and minimize your commitment to relationship marketing.

As a general rule, invest only about 20% of your total effort here. Of course, there are some special cases—perhaps you are a young attorney with few clients. Or you may be an attorney with a purely transaction based business—so you need to spend more time going directly after prospective clients.

In general, make sure your priorities are in order. Put 20% of your resources in personal marketing. Incrementally extend your reach beyond your immediate circle of contacts and acquaintances.

Here's a second lesson: Realize that we are talking about marketing your PERSONAL reputation. Your firm can only sell you so much—because people buy services from individuals NOT FIRMS. After all, to be successful you have to be known for your personal capabilities and expertise.

Now, what are the best ways to create your personal reputation? There is one overriding rule that the best business generators follow: MARKETING IS A CONTACT SPORT. The marketing that works the best is the kind that puts you in direct contact with somebody that you want to have as a client. What are the most productive ways to make marketing contact? Here are the FAB FIVE. These are the best, most proven techniques used by the best business generators.

- *Public speaking and seminars:* Done properly, public speaking is a "sales call" on a group of prospects. However, too many attorneys waste their speaking engagements by "over-educating." We'll show you how to turn speaking engagements into new business.

- *Integrated direct marketing campaigns*: A highly targeted, consistent, sustained and ongoing direct mail campaign can add lots of business to your practice. Many firms waste their money on incomplete mailing strategies.

We'll show you how to win this direct marketing game—including how to design the campaign, as well as methods for complementing the mailing with other related efforts that bolster your overall impact on the market.

- *Special events*: Finding an appealing excuse to get a gathering of prospects and clients to attend an event is a golden marketing opportunity. It gives you a chance to informally market and sell by mingling and interviewing.

- *Roundtables and special interest groups:* Informal discussion groups among peers are extremely attractive to your prospects and clients. By organizing and facilitating these groups, you can position yourself as an expert on the topic at hand. This also gives your clients a platform to "sing your praises."

- *Visible leadership positions at associations:* Another marketing tool that you should emphasize is association leadership positions. But, you have to be visible. Become the program chairman or membership director. Be a frequent speaker. Find "excuses" to meet prospective clients. In other words, WORK at it—don't simply be a passive member of the organization.

These are the proven marketing winners. Let the other firms waste time on the marketing programs that fall short again and again. Make direct contact—while others make excuses and try to take the easy way out.

SUMMARY

Let's recap what we've learned in this chapter.

- Realize that as a professional person you've already got all of the personal assets you need to create more business effectively. You're experienced at asking questions, you have the technical ability to do the work, and you're an expert diagnostician.

- To enhance your business development results, all you have to do is learn form those who excel. Emulate the best business generators—for they have developed proven techniques, success strategies and productive business building habits.

- The bottom line is that business development is simply a skill—one that can be learned & honed.

- Success isn't accidental. The main difference between top producers and those that fall short comes down to their attitudes and aptitudes towards business development.

- Problems occur when attorneys possess attitudes that limit their ability to build their practice. Instead, find a way to shift how you think about business development.

Make it a top daily priority. Squeeze it into your day—even during your busiest times. Then, aim to keep improving continually at business development.

- See yourself as an entrepreneur—one who can share the broad business perspective of your clients and prospects. Get close to your clients in the industries that you specialize in, so that you can understand their critical business concerns. Listen to them and see how you can help to alleviate their pain.

- To build your practice, it's vital that you see the marketing possibilities in each and every interaction. And, be armed with a business development goal to take control of these interactions.

- Here's the tough part. Because we're professionals and not full time salespeople, we tend to take our eye off of the "marketing and selling ball." We get wrapped up in doing the day-to-day work for our clients. It's certainly reasonable that we often put business development on the back burner and forget about it.

- So, you have to WORK at your ATTITUDE. CONSCIOUSLY, strive to think about business development in the ways that will vitalize your practice. RESOLVE to avoid the excuses for ignoring business development.

- Beyond building a strong business development attitude, you also need a systematic personal marketing plan. We find that professionals fail when they seek to market and sell their services in all of the wrong places, where they are least likely to generate more work.

- Instead, if you focus on the right marketing activities and perform these actions on a systematic, daily basis, then you'll start to produce the kind of results you desire.

- Avoid the problems that defeat the average practitioner. Remember that the most important lessons to learn from the best business generators is to work from the `inside out!' "

- This means that YOU are THE MESSAGE. You are the "product." And you are your own "product manager" and sales force. All marketing comes down to the individual. After all, clients evaluate and hire individuals NOT solely firms. Referrals are made based on personal reputations and relationships NOT firm referrals. Ultimately, nobody can market and sell your services BUT you.

- Therefore, you need a personal marketing plan. Begin by focusing on your golden opportunities. These are your top clients—along with those prospects who are "clones" of these clients.

- Then, instead of wasting enormous amounts of your valuable time marketing to strangers, develop special relationships with your clients. This should be 70–80% of your effort. **These are the people who are most important for reaching your goals.**

- Next, invest time cultivating exceptional relationships with those select professional allies both inside and outside of the firm. Go to market on a cooperative basis with your allies. Refer lots of business back and forth. Be first on each other's list of professional allies. Again, this should be about 10–15% of your plan.

- As a final step, the best business generators invest their time wisely by developing their personal reputation. They don't rely on their firm to market them. Instead, they differentiate themselves personally by publicizing the qualities and experiences that make them UNIQUE.

- Why do these strategies work? The best business developers put their success totally within their own span of control. They've achieved leverage by magnifying their efforts through creating a committed team of clients and allies who are seeking out even more opportunities for them!

- By using this approach, you concentrate on the most effective ways to create business. You won't have to become a "salesperson" who is constantly hawking yourself. You can be comfortable by being who you are. Then, look to have business come to you!

- Now, what do you do? You create a personal marketing plan of attack that duplicates the success strategies of the best business generators. Diligently follow the steps in the system and success will come.

- Our goal in this chapter was simple: to give you the most efficient, direct path to success. The one that the best business generators use—day in and day out to create the results you desire.

HOW TO FOCUS ON YOUR BEST OPPORTUNITIES: DEFINING YOUR PERSONAL MARKETING STRATEGY

INTRODUCTION

In this chapter we'll guide you to begin creating your own custom-designed personal marketing plan. You'll define the value of your services and find out which clients need your services the most. You'll find out where you can be most successful marketing your services and discover the best ways to promote yourself.

LET'S GET STARTED ON YOUR PLAN

You'll start creating your personal marketing plan by getting focused on your "golden opportunities".

What's a golden opportunity? Simply put, a golden opportunity is **finding those market needs and wants that are both most attractive to you, as well as where your chances for success are greatest.**

FOCUS helps you to keep your eye on the prize.

Focus makes your life easier and more productive—because you will make a frank appraisal of your strengths. Then, you will gear your *full efforts* on your best clients—along with a precisely defined group of realistic, achievable and profitable prospective clients.

THE PERSONAL MARKETING STRATEGY SYSTEM

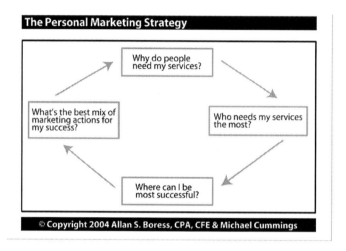

The Personal Marketing Strategy

Why do people need my services?

Who needs my services the most?

Where can I be most successful?

What's the best mix of marketing actions for my success?

© Copyright 2004 Allan S. Boress, CPA, CFE & Michael Cummings

Here's another way to look at it. See yourself as a "product" that you are bringing to market. There are four questions you need to answer before you can properly market any product or service.

Rule: You Are The Product

Question #1: Why Do People Need Your Product?

Question #2: Which Clients And Prospective Clients Need Your Product The Most?

Question #3: Where Can You Be Most Successful In Marketing Your Services?

Question #4: What's The Best Way to Promote to Your Best Prospects and Targets?

Let's review each of these inquiries in detail:

QUESTION #1: *DEFINING YOUR PERSONAL VALUE PROPOSITION:*
Why Do People Need You and Your Expertise?

First, you need to define your personal "value proposition".

What need, hurt, ache, problem, want or desire do you satisfy in your clients?

Why are they willing to part with their hard-earned dollars for your services?

Why is your blend of expertise, experience, past client engagements and industry know-how of particular value?

Do you have some special service savvy that either eliminates a client's "hurt, ache, trauma or problem" or makes their life easier?

How is your "value" distinctive and different from other "attorneys" that can satisfy this need?

By answering these questions, you are putting yourself in the buyer's shoes, which is the first step in any marketing process.

Consider the automobile industry and the product variety that the many manufacturers offer. Mini-vans, pick-up trucks, compact cars, luxury cars and sports cars all serve different customer needs, wants and desires. Each product has a variety of attributes that solves a different problem set for their customer.

This first step in your marketing process results in a self-examination of your core strengths: technical, client service, industry understanding, and functional service know-how.

How are your clients better off through your service?

What benefits do they garner from your services?

How would they describe these benefits in their own words?

Why do they hire you instead of another attorney?

Later in this chapter, we'll guide you through an exercise to answer these questions for your practice.

QUESTION #2: DEFINING YOUR "IDEAL CLIENT"

Second, you must find the groups of clients and prospects that have the greatest need for what you have to offer.

How can you define this group?

Do they vary by industry? By business structure? Size? Geography? Tax complexities? Degree of computerization? Sophistication of internal staff?

In marketing, *the process of answering these questions is called "market segmentation."*

The purpose of market segmentation is to precisely define those groups and sub-groups of companies or individuals with the best potential for you. Precisely defining these market segments leads to more efficient, targeted and successful marketing efforts.

Take the automobile analogy once again. For example, lower cost "sporty" models like the Ford Mustang appeal to younger people starting out on their first job. Therefore, everything about these cars and the corresponding marketing campaigns are geared to appeal to this market segment: flashier colors, sporty styling, first-time buyer programs, and lower prices. Youth-oriented advertising is emphasized on TV and radio programs that have the right youth-oriented demographics—usually with an upbeat message backed by popular rock music.

Contrast this with the marketing of mini-vans. The target market segment for those vehicles is growing families. Therefore, auto companies promote those product qualities that will appeal to the decision-makers in these families (often the wife and mother in the family: the person who will be using the vehicle the most). Roominess, reliability, the safety of young passengers, low maintenance, and ease of driving are their concerns. Also, the advertising is geared towards television programs that they tend to watch, magazines they most likely read, applied with a more sedate and sensible promotional message than that geared to young and single people.

What do you think would happen to the sales of mini-vans and sporty models if they were marketed generically to everybody?

This same segmentation process applies to your practice. As you review the clients you already serve, we're certain that you'll see several "market segments."

This means that there are a few groups of businesses or individuals with common attributes, facing the same types of problems.

There is a reason that these clients selected you and stayed clients. You are serving a need, want, desire, trauma, ache or hurt they have in a way that they value and trust.

By understanding this segmentation, *you can define and target the market niche that needs your service most and best respects your track record and service capabilities.* Again, the more precise and narrow your definition of these pockets of opportunities, just like in the automobile business, the more effective and efficient you'll be in converting business.

QUESTION #3: *EXPLOITING YOUR MARKET SHARE ADVANTAGES:*
Where Can You Be Most Successful In Marketing Your Services?

Third, you need to know where you should be marketing.

Each firm or practitioner will have both assets and liabilities in pursuing a market opportunity. *The goal is to go where your strengths are greatest and exploit this opportunity to the maximum.*

In marketing terminology, this is referred to as *exploiting "market share advantages"* to grow.

In plain English, this means building on your past success for incremental business growth. Or using your strengths and advantages to attract more clients like your best existing clients.

This also makes sense from a client's or prospect's point of view. Pretend that you are the CFO of a hospital looking for a law firm: Which firms would you ask to propose? Wouldn't you want a firm that understood the special problems that your hospital was up against? How could you tell if a firm specialized in your type of hospital?

Exploiting "market share advantages" will give you more opportunities to sell your services.

If you were the CFO, it's clear that you'd look for a firm that served a number of hospitals that you considered to be just like *yours*. You would first think about any attorneys who you know personally and then you'd ask your colleagues at other hospitals who they have as their attorneys. You'd find out which partners served these hospitals and ask for further references or client lists. In this way, you'd be seeking evidence that you were getting qualified candidates to propose, so that you would receive the best service, superior advice, efficient work, and reduce your risk of a poor decision.

Doesn't this selection process only make sense? How difficult would it be to get this engagement if you served only one other hospital, or none at all (little or no "market share advantage")?

Recognize that this same buying dynamic applies to your practice as well. It's easier to grow in those areas where you are already successful and strong (assuming there is still room for growth). This is also where your referral base and service reputation is most potent.

So what do you do if you are in a maturing line of business or a dying practice area? Each year place a bet on a new industry or service area that you feel has next generation growth possibilities. Pick something closely related to your core technical expertise or another "area of pain" that is impacting your core client base. Even if you only have an engagement or two, you can be an expert in the eyes of your clients. Take a CLE course (Continuing Legal Education). Find somebody who is successful in this area and learn their approach. Think of your service expertise in the same way you think about your financial portfolio. Allocate some time and money to an aggressive growth area.

Thus, in our personal market planning work with you, we will help you to build this disciplined focus into your personal success strategy.

QUESTION #4: WHAT IS THE BEST WAY TO REACH & CONVERT CLIENTS?
Lastly, in bringing your "product" (you) to market, you need to know the best ways to promote it.

The selection of your target market niches will guide and define the rest of your marketing action plan. Each marketing action that you consider must be screened against the following standard:

Will this marketing action attract the highest priority client or prospect that I desire?

If it doesn't produce this result, then why would you want to invest ANY time or money in this marketing effort?

Please realize that the selection of your priority clients and target prospects will guide the rest of your plan. Your target niche will determine what kind of marketing makes the most sense. After all, you wouldn't market to a large corporation in the same way that you'd market to a contractor.

In marketing terminology, there are different marketing *"channels."* This means that there are distinct vehicles for promoting yourself that are different for each market segment. They belong to different associations, read industry specific periodicals, and attend different conferences.

Also, different market segments respond to a different mix of marketing tools. It's difficult to get attorneys to respond to a "direct mailing campaign"—because they are drowning in paper. But, they do respond to direct referrals by other attorneys that they respect. Or, it's possible to generate work by speaking at LEGAL Association meetings or via Continuing Education Programs.

So, we need to define this proper mix of tools for you—based on your priorities.

THE PRACTICAL VALUE OF FOCUS FOR YOU

The last section conveyed the marketing imperatives for focus. But, there are also pragmatic reasons for a strict focus for your marketing effort.

First, *you can't be all things to all people.* In fact, the more generic or commonplace you look—the less valuable you seem. Conversely, the more distinctive and unique you appear—the more value you project.

Second, *if your marketing effort is scattered and diffuse, then your impact will be weak.* Without a strong focus, many attorneys end up in running in circles—chasing any opportunity that looks like a possibility. With focus, you get a strong, sustained and consistent exertion on a clear, precise target.

Third, *your competition is becoming more specialized and focused.* Niche marketing is now the standard of success in the profession. It's no secret that the big law firms invest significantly in their industry programs and service line teams. These firms want to be fully up to speed on their clients' specific business challenges. Also, they invest in marketing programs geared specifically towards these industry/service priorities.

What the big firms do doesn't apply to you? Even mid-sized and smaller practices are becoming highly specialized. Increasingly, you see partners that concentrate their full time and effort on a single industry or service line. One New York firm boasts of fourteen partners devoted only to Internet and high-tech start-up companies. Just like medicine, the law profession is quickly becoming much more specialized and focused. It's your choice: You can get with the program now, be a leader and grab a bigger piece of the market share while your competition is still sleeping, or wait until they grab your market share.

Fourth, *you don't have the time to promote to a wide variety of market segments.* What's the most precious resource for any attorney? It's your time. After all, you make money by billing your time. So, you can't waste time and energy by chasing opportunities that aren't likely to go anywhere.

Another way of looking at focus is as a process of *disciplined priority setting.* Even if you have the experience and expertise to serve a wide variety of industries or types of businesses—you simply don't have the time. Therefore, you have to look at your strengths and your best opportunities. Then, keep concentrated on your top two or three market priorities.

In this way, you always keep striving for those opportunities that mean the most to you—instead of furiously chasing clients or prospects that are less valuable.

Fifth, it's much easier to get referrals when you know exactly who and what you want your clients to be!

Focus makes it more likely to receive referrals because it is simpler for someone to access a specific "file" in their mind rather than an entire "data base."

Perhaps you asked someone to refer you to someone who might need an attorney. There's a problem: that person must now access every person (every "file" in their "data base" of people they know) in their entire mind to see if they know anyone for you. That's too much work!

However, with the power of focus, you can be much more specific with the referrals you request. You've limited the number of people or companies to a smaller group, but have increased the odds they will comply with your request. *It's easier for someone to refer a client to you if they know exactly what you are looking for as it limits the number of files in their memory to a specific category.*

We'll cover how, when and where to ask for referrals in a later chapter.

Sixth and finally, *focus makes you more distinctive and valuable in the eyes of your clients and prospects.* There's an old adage in the goal-setting business: "It's better to be a meaningful specific than a wandering generality." The same is true for your marketing strategy.

Let's look at another analogy. There's a concept in marketing called "brand loyalty". This means that you are likely to recognize a particular brand (like Crest toothpaste, Coke or Tide detergent). More importantly, if you like that product and appreciate the results it provides, you will be willing to pay a higher price for that perceived value.

In other aisles of the supermarket, you see commodities. Think about the "generic" aisle—where there are no "brands." Perhaps you are attracted to the low cost and see no additional value in the price for a recognized brand. Or consider another commodity like "produce." It's likely that you don't look for a particular brand of apples, lettuce or asparagus.

Do you want to be perceived as a "generic attorney?" What will happen to your fees if you do? You want to become a recognizable and valuable personal brand—it adds value to what you do.

A more precise, clear and narrow description of your personal service value will make you more distinctive in the marketplace. Instead of being just an "attorney," be perceived as a "specialist in family-owned wholesale distributors in Broward County". Or specialize in asset valuation for high-income divorce cases.

Focus is the proper way to *position yourself* in the market place. And, we'll work with you to define this personal focus for you.

WHY MANY ATTORNEYS RESIST FOCUS IN THEIR PERSONAL MARKETING STRATEGY

Right about now, it's likely that a few of you are resisting this idea of focus. You might feel that you'd be limiting your opportunity due to a restricted point of view. Instead, you might believe that the more general your marketing strategy—being everything to everybody—the broader your potential would be for new business. Conversely, the stricter the focus—the fewer the target prospects that will be in your sights.

Also, if you look at the technical nature of the work that you do, in many cases you may see few differences in the technical content of the work that is performed from what others carry out for their clients. Therefore, you may be wondering, why should you market differently if your clients have similar problems, concerns and compliance requirements?

Finally, as an individual or a sole practitioner, you may be thinking that you can't afford the luxury of focus. After all, you may be serving a wide variety of clients and see potential in a variety of markets. You may feel that you need to be a generalist by the very nature of your business.

In our programs and consulting, we run into these objections to marketing focus quite often. And, we only have one answer: you really may not have a choice.

Why? *Because clients and prospects CARE about your focus.* Although they differ in degree, they value relevant knowledge and specific expertise in their business.

WHY CLIENTS VALUE FOCUSED ATTORNEYS

There is ONE overwhelming, fundamental principle in effective marketing: *the client is king.* To win and keep their business, we must all play by the rules and values that clients set without compromising our professional standards.

To compete for the attention and interest of client decision-makers, and ultimately to get and keep their work, *you must be tuned into their wavelength.* Study the top business producers in the profession, as we have for the past twenty years, and you'll realize that *they excel at seeing the world through their clients' eyes.*

This is one reason that rainmakers excel at business development. They see themselves not only as attorneys, but also as entrepreneurs like many of their clients. Therefore, they relate well to their clients. They thrive on the client's rules of the game.

Experience proves, and market research confirms, that CLIENTS VALUE FOCUSED attorneys. Clients look for attorneys with an in-depth understanding of their business or personal financial challenges. They want an expert who can quickly solve the trauma that they might be facing. They see an expert as being more efficient in serving their needs. They believe that a specialist can get up to speed on the situation rapidly without spinning their wheels struggling to learn their business.

Also, it's been proven that the quality of rapport and personal chemistry is central to success in winning a client's business. Consequently, the more you understand about a clients' business, the more likely you will be able to empathize and relate to the client.

Moreover, you can ask more insightful and reasoned questions that will lead to a more thorough diagnosis and sale.

All of these factors combine to make focus critical to your ability to build the kind of personal chemistry that your clients and ideal prospects will value.

Again, this only makes sense. Let's step into a buyer's shoes for a second. Think about how you select and invest in the services of a doctor. If you hurt your back severely, whom would you go see? Anybody? Of course, you'd most likely go to an orthopedic specialist to get a sound diagnosis and expert remedy.

Have we lost you here? Maybe your clients only put a premium on how little they pay you. Why is that, *really?* Simply because they're cheap? Or because there is "so much competition" or the "economy?"

Or is it possibly because they don't see the value in having you help them with their business? Is it possible that your clients don't see you as anything more than an expensive, necessary evil? Then, why is that so?

Take a minute, step back, and consider what is the most important thing in your business client's life. Is it his family? His health? Or might it be his business?

Although we can't speak for you, we've found that, especially with business owners, often the most important thing in their lives is their business. It's "their baby." They want it to be healthy and grow. Do people beat their baby's doctors up over fees? We think not.

Maybe you've received so much fee resistance in the past because your clients and prospective clients view you as a generic attorney, with little or no ability or desire to help them with their business. *That's where the power of focus comes in.*

Remember, the bottom line is that your clients and prospects must put a premium on the depth of your understanding of their business and personal needs for you to be most successful.

Focus and specialization is the best way that you can meet this goal. Therefore, it has to be the driving force in your personal marketing strategy.

WHERE DOES BUSINESS COME FROM?

We've got to cover one more key to marketing success.

Let's analyze the best business generators once again. Remember, everything we cover in the course is modeled on how the best business generators, in small and large firms, succeed.

Now, we'll look at how the best build their practice. Where does their new business come from?

This is no accident. Forging strong, vital relationships with clients is a prerequisite for success in the profession. 50% of your new business should come strictly from existing clients, in the form of additional services and referrals from them.

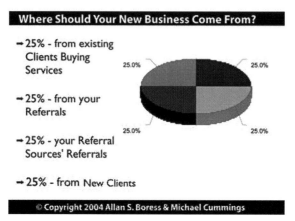

If you excel at this and stay close to your client's business, they will see you almost as an extension of their company resources. Consequently, they'll repeatedly hire you for additional work, special engagements and consultative advice as the need arises. Also, they'll actively refer and recommend you—leading to even more business.

Next in importance are Allies. As with their top clients, the best business generators reap a lot of business from close, committed relationships with attorneys, bankers, insurance brokers, securities people, bonding companies, etc. In effect, your close allies must act like your external "sales force"—securing for you a steady stream of referrals that contribute to your growth.

The final component is direct prospecting and marketing to prospective clients, or "strangers." This encompasses seminars, public speaking, mailings, association involvement, advertising, your web site, etc. Immediate personal contact and disciplined follow-through is essential after direct marketing and means little without it.

WHAT DOES THIS MEAN FOR YOU?

First, if approximately 50% of your new business should come from clients and their referrals, then where should you invest 50% of your marketing attention and effort? That's right—with your current clients . . . *because they are your most important business building asset.*

Second, what kinds of prospective clients are your best existing clients likely to refer you to? Of course . . . people just like them—either in the same business, at the same income or social level, or facing the same personal challenges. Again, <u>that's where focus pays off.</u>

Third, allies are the next important resource. A lot of time, investment and marketing attention are required to nurture these strong alliances. With clients and allies spreading word of mouth marketing, <u>you create a sustained force in the marketplace.</u>

Fourth, when most attorneys think about marketing, THEY FOCUS THE GREAT MAJORITY (75% or more) OF THEIR EFFORT AND MARKETING DOLLARS ON MARKETING CONTACTS INTENDED TO GENERATE NEW CONTACTS WITH STRANGERS! And then they complain, "Marketing doesn't pay off."

Instead, we recommend that you invest 75% of your marketing effort on building strong personal relationships with Allies and clients. Then, you can build off of this success with concerted, focused marketing campaigns.

Of course, there are some exceptions. If you don't have any current clients, then you have to hustle harder with referral sources and direct marketing to prospects. Also, if you sell primarily independent engagements, you'll also have to emphasize more direct marketing, because that's a transaction-oriented business. But, for the conventional attorney with an established practice, the above standards apply.

We now move to building these guidelines into your definition of your focus.

DEFINING YOUR PERSONAL FOCUS

Who should you be targeting for marketing efforts?

Here are the THREE CRITICAL RULES of personal marketing FOCUS:

Rule #1: *Focus first on your BEST clients.*

Rule #2: *Focus next on PROSPECTIVE CLIENTS who are "CLONES" of your BEST CLIENTS.*

Rule #3: *Focus an ALLIES who can GET YOU MORE BUSINESS FROM CLIENTS AND REFERRALS INTO "CLONES" OF YOUR BEST CLIENTS.*

Rule #4: *Focus on direct marketing to those places where YOU CAN REACH CLONED CLIENTS AND REFERRALS OF THOSE KINDS OF PEOPLE.*

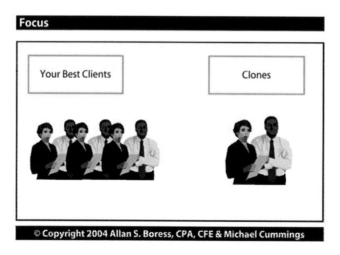

Doesn't this appear logical? We've found that this is the best way to focus yourself. Why? *Because you were able to attract and keep your best clients for a reason:* mainly due to your service expertise, understanding of their business, ability to help these clients succeed and your personal relationship with them. Said another way, your personal strengths are the reason that you've retained and prospered with these top clients.

Accordingly, where can your strengths be best directed for optimal results? TO PROSPECTS WHO ARE SIMILAR TO YOUR TOP CLIENTS.

By playing to your strengths, you increase your chances for success. Why stray away from your best market niches? Unless the market is so thoroughly saturated and/or you can't serve these target clients at a profit, let your competitors waste their time and diffuse their marketing impact.

Stay focused—and concentrate your full energy and marketing investment on a smaller number of high priority market niches.

BUILDING FOCUS INTO YOUR PERSONAL MARKETING STRATEGY

Now, let's custom-tailor these ideas for YOUR practice.

We'll do this in the form of a brainstorming exercise. There are no concrete right or wrong answers for this exercise. Instead, the point is to be creative, introspective and coldly analytical. You may want to try this exercise several times over a period of a week or so, and you might care to get some further input from trusted professional colleagues, allies that you respect, or even clients who know you well.

BRAINSTORMING EXERCISE

To perform this exercise you'll need a list of your clients. Ideally, use a list that rank orders your clients from highest to lowest in terms of professional fees over the past twelve months or last fiscal year.

To do this exercise correctly, we recommend that you use a spreadsheet that lists the client's name in the first column. This leaves a lot of room for brainstorming.

STEP #1: LIST YOUR CLIENTS IN DESCENDING ORDER BY FEES.

You're going to concentrate on the top end of the list, those clients who generate the majority of your fees. While there are no hard and fast rules, we suggest you view your clients with the classic 80/20 rule in mind. Focus on the top 20% of your clients that generate 80% (or the majority) of your revenues. Highlight this segment of your client base by drawing a line that separates them from the rest.

STEP #2: SCAN DOWN THE REST OF THE LIST.

Look for any clients who meet one or more of the following conditions:

Their future fee potential will put them into your top 20% within the next year or two

They are a superb referral source

You are providing them with a special advisory service that you want to emphasize within your top 20%

Place an "X" next to those that apply.

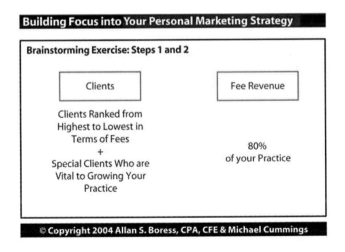

Building Focus into Your Personal Marketing Strategy

Brainstorming Exercise: Steps 1 and 2

| Clients | Fee Revenue |

Clients Ranked from Highest to Lowest in Terms of Fees
+
Special Clients Who are Vital to Growing Your Practice

80% of your Practice

STEP #3: CONDUCT A "CLUSTER ANALYSIS"

In this step, you'll be using a brainstorming technique called "cluster analysis". In Step # 4 you will segregate your clients with similar characteristics into several distinct, precisely defined groups ("clusters").

Your first goal here in Step # 3 is to come up with the categories into which you can then "cluster" your clients. Start working your way down the list, beginning with your largest client.

Next to the client's name, write a brief description of this client's business. Try to make your description as specific as possible. Essentially, answer the following question: "What is unique about this client's business?"

Remember two rules as you do this analysis: be brief and be creative. Combine as many attributes as you need to be as precise as possible.

Here are some descriptive guidelines for BUSINESS CLIENTS:

A "micro-specific" definition of their industry.

A description of their customer base

Products/services they sell.

Their size in terms of revenue or fee growth.

Their location/geographic diversion or concentration.

Stage of growth or maturity of the business.

Ownership structure (e.g.: family owned; closely-held; second generation).

Significant transactions they face (selling off the company; transferring the business to the next generation; getting ready for an IPO, etc.)

Age of the owners/major executives.

Top two or three business challenges that the company is facing.

Recovery of fees and speed of payment.

Building Focus into Your Personal Marketing Strategy

Brainstorming Exercise: Step 3

ABC Company	Large Wholesale Distributor with Ownership Recently Transferred to the Next Generation
XYZ Company	High Tech Startup with Significant Planning & Consulting Needs

Here are some descriptive guidelines for INDIVIDUAL CLIENTS:

Level of income.

Key personal financial planning challenges (e.g.: estate planning, education funding, pension plans, potential for financial services).

Stage of life.

Key tax and estate considerations.

Source of income.

Nature of their profession.

Where they are located.

Recovery on fees and speed of payment.

Here's a rule of thumb as you complete this brainstorming exercise: **Do it at a brisk pace.** Jot down the principal phrases that do the best job of describing the client. Then quickly move on to the next. But, combine as many factors that you need to precisely define the client.

Work your way down the list until you covered ALL the top clients.

STEP #4: GROUP SIMILAR CLIENTS INTO A "CLUSTER"

Your objective in this step is to group similar clients into a cluster, or a "market niche." The purpose of this step is to link together clients into as distinctive and homogeneous clusters as possible.

Here are some guidelines for "clustering":

1. Begin with industry-oriented or lines of business groupings

Continue from there to re-describe or improve your description of each cluster (make it more clear, more concise, etc.-see Step #4 example). If clustering by industry doesn't work out, then use ownership structure (i.e. family held).

2. You can put a particular business client into more than one cluster

For example, you could put a client into an industry cluster. Then, you might also put them into one of your service line groupings, such as succession planning. Be as creative as you need to be to place clients into as many clusters as they "qualify" for in your estimation.

3. If you are lumping far too many clients into one cluster, take a closer look at the cluster

Work hard to find differences and distinctions within the cluster to see what sub-groupings appear logical. Look for additional descriptions that can create meaningful segments within the cluster.

4. Alternatively, if you have too many clusters (10–12), you have two choices.

You may leave them as is, because you may have that kind of diversity within your base. Or, you can look for ways to combine clusters.

STEP #5: RANK THE CLUSTERS IN TERMS OF YOUR TOP PRIORITY

To maximize your marketing effectiveness and profitability, you are going to want to focus on your top priority clusters. Look at the clusters and evaluate how much service potential exists within the client segment inside the cluster grouping. In determining your rankings of priority, ask yourself the following questions:

- What are my current fees at these clients?

- Has this grown or shrunk over the past 2 years?

- Do they actively seek my advice and counsel?

- Do we provide a good deal of consultative service to this cluster?

- Are any of these clients good referral sources?

- Do I have some strong allies at this client (e.g. their bankers or attorneys)? Have they given me referrals to prospective clients?

- Do I understand these businesses well? Do I also have good rapport with these clients?

- Are their businesses growing or shrinking? Is the marketplace for their goods or services growing or shrinking?

Realize that this isn't intended to be a hard and fast quantitative analysis. Instead, use your instinct and judgement. Then, force yourself to assign a rank. Don't settle for a tie. Make a clear decision.

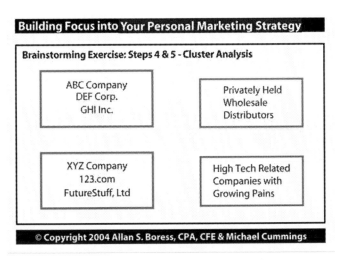

Building Focus into Your Personal Marketing Strategy

Brainstorming Exercise: Steps 4 & 5 - Cluster Analysis

ABC Company DEF Corp. GHI Inc.	Privately Held Wholesale Distributors
XYZ Company 123.com FutureStuff, Ltd	High Tech Related Companies with Growing Pains

© Copyright 2004 Allan S. Boress, CPA, CFE & Michael Cummings

STEP #6: TEST YOUR CLUSTER ANALYSIS

This cluster analysis is essential to your personal marketing strategy. So, it's vital that you test it. Review your cluster analysis with a professional colleague that you trust. Try to select someone with a solid understanding of business development. Explain your top segments and get their reaction.

Then tap into the expertise of your clients. Meet and interview a few of them over lunch, perhaps. Ask them which industry or business associations they frequent. Do they read specialty magazines or newsletters? Where do they go to get the latest information? What conventions do they attend? If you feel comfortable, review your description of their cluster. How would the client modify or enhance your description?

STEP #7: STEP BACK AND TAKE ACCOUNT OF YOUR FEEDBACK.

Review this cluster analysis at a future date and refine your descriptions as needed. For comparison, take a look at the following cluster analysis performed by one of our clients. Notice how specific and distinctive the descriptions are in this example. How do your descriptions compare to the exhibit?

Now you can perceive the value of focus. Notice how easily an ally will understand who your target clients are so that he or she could make an introduction for you.

Building Focus into Your Personal Marketing Strategy

Priority Niches Market Worksheet

Real Estate
1. Large established home builders
2. New, small growing builders in Kane County
3. Older owners who need age-based pension plan

Divorce Cases
1. Kane County divorce attorneys representing spouses of high-income individuals
2. Clients pay in a timely manner
3. Charge premium rates
4. Get spouse's tax work later

© Copyright 2004 Allan S. Boress, CPA, CFE & Michael Cummings

STEP #8: DEVELOPING YOUR 30 SECOND COMMERCIAL

Here's the final step in this exercise. Select your top two clusters. Create a thirty-second commercial for yourself.

Remember that the purpose of <u>focus</u> is to make you as distinctive and unique as possible in the eyes of prospects and referral sources.

Now is the time to develop your "thirty-second commercial."

This commercial will be your "introduction" when you have the opportunity to meet your ideal prospective clients, or to important referral sources who can introduce you to your target client.

WHY A COMMERCIAL IS IMPORTANT

The notion of a personal commercial was first drummed home to us when Rita, an attorney, became our client many years ago.

Rita had been a practicing attorney for over sixteen years at that point and was still struggling with her practice. During those previous years she had been active in a number of organizations in the city where she lived, all of which were in some way related to her specialty, advertising law.

Rita was particularly perturbed about never receiving a single referral, introduction or case from her many contacts amongst the hundreds of members of the Advertising Club (a major organization) she belonged to. She had even been president.

Fortunately, we had some other clients who were also members and active in the organization. We asked them if they knew Rita, and they all did. NOT ONE OF THEM KNEW THAT RITA WAS AN EXPERT AT ADVERTISING LAW!

Why? *Because she had never told them.* Whenever she introduced herself, she would say that she was an attorney. How do you introduce yourself?

We've learned from the Best Business Generators in the professions that you always have to take the occasion to tell people what you do whenever presented with the opportunity because one never knows which person you meet will turn into a client or a referral source.

Personal marketing is a sort of grand treasure hunt. You can't know, or prejudge, who can or will help you until they know what you do. So you have to keep "broadcasting" your message when given the opportunity everywhere you go, just in case. Referrals and business come from the strangest places.

Within one year of personalizing a commercial for Rita, she had sixteen new cases and three solid referral sources in that one organization.

Also, your commercial gives the other person an opportunity to ask you questions, above and beyond what could be expected if you say, "I'm an attorney."

DOES EVERYONE KNOW WHAT YOU DO?

Let's imagine that you are attending an important networking event. You have the chance to meet face-to-face with an ideal prospective client—one who is in your highest priority market niche.

What impression do you want to make? How do you want to be remembered?

WRITING YOUR COMMERCIAL

In this segment we will walk you through the process of creating your own commercial.

Yes, you can have more than one commercial depending on the situation. If one of your market niches is estate planning, and you are speaking at a retirement village to a group of senior citizens, your commercial will be different than if you want to promote this same service to a group of business-owners at an association meeting.

For our purposes right now, choose your highest priority market niche.

Here are the elements you need to have in place for a good thirty-second commercial:

1. Review the description of your target niche.

2. The first rule is to be brief, but descriptive.

3. Don't start your commercial with "I'm an attorney." It's too generic. Think about the last person who introduced himself or herself to you as an "insurance agent" or "personal financial planner." What was your reaction?

STEP #1: COMPLETE THE FOLLOWING SENTENCE: "I SPECIALIZE IN WORKING WITH.............."

Review what you wrote. Is it brief? Specific? Accurate? Interesting

STEP #2: NOW WORK ON THE NEXT SENTENCE.

Select two types of services that you offer to your highest priority market segment that you described above.

Think about the most pressing problems that you help them solve. WE DON'T WANT YOU TO DESCRIBE WHAT YOU DO FOR THEM.

For example, you don't want to say you do tax planning or employment contracts.

INSTEAD, WE WANT YOU TO DESCRIBE THE URGENT PROBLEMS AND PERSONAL TRAUMA THEY FACE. Like, minimizing their taxes to *preserve their cash* flow; or setting up pension plans leading *to a secure* retirement; or working with companies to *maximize the effectiveness* of their organizations. Or, protecting the vital intellectual property assets of their business. Remember, the client or prospect doesn't care about the process (features), HE OR SHE ONLY CARES ABOUT THE SELFISH RESULTS (the advantage, or consequence of what you do—the avoidance or alleviation of nagging problems; the improvement of previous circumstances).

Now, it's your turn. Describe what problems you solve. How does your service make your clients better off?

I help these clients to….

Problem #1/client advantage:

Problem #2/client advantage:

STEP #3: TEST IT OUT.

Run this thirty-second commercial by your clients and colleagues. Ask them how clear it is. Does it sound "right"? How could it be enhanced?

Examples of Thirty-Second Commercials

Poor Examples: (too limiting and boring)

"I'm an attorney."

"I do tax work."

"I am an employment law specialists."

"I specialize in product liability law."

"I consult on trademark issues."

More Poor Examples: (too generic)

"I work with small business in their start up phase . . . "

"I work with manufacturers, wholesale distributors, non-profit organizations, contractors, developers, banks, hospitals, municipal governments . . . "

GOOD EXAMPLES THAT ARE PROVEN WINNERS:

(used with permission from our clients)

"I'm Jill Swill and I'm a partner with the law firm of Joe Blow and Associates. I'm in the business of helping senior citizens to organize their estates and achieve a secure retirement."

"I'm Maggie Baggie and I'm an associate with the law firm of Marin and Moron and I specialize in working with software companies to protect their intellectual property assets from theft by competitors and hackers."

"I'm Archie Becker. I have my own law practice and we work with women facing a divorce to ensure a fair and equitable settlement from a financial standpoint."

"I'm Chris Bliss and I'm a partner with the firm of Church and Lurch. I work with non-profit organizations to attract funding through living will and trust programs."

"I'm Molly Ringworm. I have my own consulting practice and I specialize in developing pension-funding strategies that minimizes tax exposure and maximizes the benefits to the owners."

"I'm Stacy Lacy. Our firm works with family businesses to make sure that they have a business transition plan in place in the event of retirement and illness."

"I'm Rick Slick and I work in the financial planning group of Super Freak LLC. We work with family held businesses to ensure that they don't send one dime more than necessary of their hard-earned money to the federal or state government in this lifetime or the next."

At first glance, they look a bit cumbersome, don't they? The point is that they work. In every example above, our client can point to business created and referrals received because they struck a cord from the get-go in a conversation. Each short commercial broadcasts a distinct, targeted message, which can be changed depending on who one is talking to.

Sometimes, people will use your commercial as a jumping off point for other services. "Stacy Lacy," above, related the situation of a new client she met at a local business card exchange meeting using her commercial above. When she said ". . . business transition plan, etc." her future client remarked: "Don't you do any taxes? We've got a problem with the IRS." At which point, she responded that she indeed had a great deal of successful experience with the IRS. Stacy set the appointment right there and secured a new client.

CONCLUSION
Let's look back at what you've accomplished in this chapter.

In essence, you've built the foundation of your personal marketing strategy and action plan through FOCUS.

Now, you recognize that clients and prospective buyers value a FOCUSED ATTORNEY—one with an in-depth understanding of their business and their personal challenges. Since client and prospects RULE the marketing game—you need to FOCUS in a way that they can perceive and appreciate.

Next, you also realized that you must play to your strengths. So, you took an INSIDE-OUT look at the power of your advantages. Starting with your best clients, you discovered, or confirmed, the different pockets of STRENGTHS you possess based on the type of clients that you ALREADY serve.

By defining your market niche, you've seen how you can extend your success by targeting CLONES of your best clients. These targets will most likely see and appreciate the value of your experience.

You then made some decisions and set priorities. Through a disciplined self-assessment of your strengths and opportunities, you've selected those niches where you have the best chance for success.

In other words, you are now FOCUSED. But, realize that building your personal marketing strategy is a "living" process—you'll find different, clearer and more precise ways to focus as you get further information and feedback from your marketing efforts.

That's okay, because you now know why focus is critical. And the more focused you become over time, the better your chances of success.

Finally, you created a short "commercial" for yourself; a way to introduce yourself to someone so that they know exactly what you do and what you are looking for, you never know where you will bump into a prospective client or referral source.

Now, let's move on and continue building your personal action plan to get and keep your top priority clients and prospects.

SUMMARY

- In developing your personal marketing plan start by focusing on your golden opportunities.

- "Focus" helps you to keep your eye on the prize.

- In marketing, the process of defining those groups and sub-groups of companies or individuals with the best potential for you is called "market segmentation".

- The goal in legal marketing is to go where your strengths are greatest and exploit this opportunity to the maximum. This is referred to as exploiting "market share advantages".

- In marketing terminology, there are different marketing "channels." This means that there are distinct vehicles for promoting yourself that are different for each market segment.

- Different market segments respond to a different mix of marketing tools.

- Focus is the proper way to position yourself in the market place.

- Focus is important to you because:

    - You can't be all things to all people

    - If your marketing effort is scattered and diffuse, then your impact will be weak

    - Your competition is becoming more specialized and focused

    - You don't have the time to promote to a wide variety of market segments

    - It is a means of disciplined priority-setting

    - It's much easier to get referrals when you know exactly who and what you want your clients to be

- It makes you more distinctive and valuable in the eyes of your clients and prospects

- Additional business needs to come from clients and their referrals (approximately 50%), your allies (approximately 25%), and strangers (25%)

- Most law firms invest the majority of their marketing time, effort and money on marketing to those least likely to buy—strangers

- Cluster your clients to determine your top priorities for marketing

- You never know where business will come from, so be prepared with a short commercial message

CHAPTER 6

THE ART OF MARKETING TO YOUR EXISTING CLIENTS

INTRODUCTION AND PURPOSE OF THIS CHAPTER

Most attorneys miss the proverbial boat when it comes to marketing additional services to their existing clients. Why? We find that some legal professionals are afraid to discuss follow up work or related services for a variety of reasons—some have tried and failed, some don't have the time, and most simply don't know how.

The top producers in our profession know that there is "gold" in their client relationship that you must "mine."

Instead of investing the majority of their precious marketing monies and efforts into doing business with strangers, they market to their existing clients. That means they keep their eyes open and constantly explore new ways of helping their clients be more successful and protected.

If a client purchases a service from another attorney (an intruder) instead of from you, not only have you lost business you should have sold, you have infected the relationship with someone who may be intent on having their alliance partner replace you as the client's counsel. Therefore, it behooves you to take all of the ideas presented in this book on how best to market your services, and yourself, and apply them first to your existing clients.

This chapter will show you how to use packaging to make your intangible services more tangible to your clients. It will also discuss the timing of marketing to clients and how to keep your clients happy.

USE PACKAGING TO MARKET SERVICES

The purpose of marketing a tangible item, such as a car, is to sell it immediately. The purpose of marketing an intangible service is to provide the *opportunity* to sell something or expand a relationship. Pontiac builds excitement! (We thought they built cars.) People pay far more for Ralph Lauren's Polo shirt because of the caché that surrounds the brand. (Caché is an intangible.) AT&T wants you to see its generic long-distance service (electric impulses traveling over fiber optic lines) as different and better than MCI's and Sprint's identical service (electric impulses traveling over fiber optic lines) by coming "home to AT&T." Michelin doesn't spend forever telling you how great their tires are, where they're made, and what they're made of. They put babies crawling on tires to drive the message home.

But that's when you're marketing a tangible item.

Marketing Truth. The secret to marketing an intangible service is to make it as tangible as possible.

Marketing an intangible service, even to a client, is more difficult than marketing a tangible product by the very nature of the item—it's invisible! It's a service; there's nothing to feel, touch, see, or smell. And, there can be a fear of endless fees—a money pit situation—where the service never ends because the job's not finished yet.

So, it's vital to package your services to successfully market them: make them easier to buy, make it simpler for the buyer to "put their arms around" the service, to be able to see it and get a distinct picture of what it will do for them. This packaging removes much of the fear of buying the service.

Let's look at a couple examples of successful packaging of intangible services. Fidelity Funds changed the profession of "investment advice" forever by the way they market and sell their mutual funds.

Thirty years ago, if you wanted to invest you would sit down with a security broker and he or she would analyze your situation and come back with recommendations. Fidelity revolutionized that professional service by packaging their advice (buy this fund) into many separate, easily identifiable "products." If you are interested in "growth," you can buy their "growth fund." If you desire to diversify some of your assets overseas, you can purchase one of their international funds.

Fidelity has done such a great job "productizing" their professional services, that people today give their precious money to total strangers 24 hours a day to invest for them with other total strangers.

The beauty of packaging is that the easier you make it for someone to grasp what you do, the more likely they are to buy it and see the value inherent in it. We must change the way the service provider sees what they do in order to market it more effectively. We must *stop* seeing what we do as billable hours and *start* seeing our work as a tangible offering that has definable value. This, by the way, we can charge more for as a package, rather than just hours, as the client is accustomed to buying other tangible and intangible items in this way.

You can package any service to make it more tangible.

The client will always perceive more value if the service is productized as we instruct you to do and packaged services are the best way to educate everyone in the firm as to the various services that are offered.

FOUR-STEP PROCESS TO MARKET TO EXISTING CLIENTS

The only difference between marketing services to new clients and marketing new services to existing, satisfied clients is that marketing to satisfied clients should be much easier. Existing satisfied clients have already made a decision to do business with you, which is the hardest hurdle to overcome in any sale. And rainmakers know that the more business they sell to their existing clients, the more secure the relationship is.

The steps to do this are:

Step #1. Audit and prioritize relationships

Step #2. Package intangible services.

Step #3. Prescribe now–operate later.

Step #4. Keep the client happy.

STEP #1. AUDIT AND PRIORITIZE RELATIONSHIPS

Review the work you did in the last chapter. Select a short list of your clients with the most potential. Think about the decision-makers at the client. Concentrate on 2–3 real life examples as you go through this process.

STEP #2. PACKAGE INTANGIBLE SERVICES

Productizing helps remove the fear of buying professional services for the buyer who may have experienced, or fears, a money pit situation, wherein seemingly endless amounts (often not discussed) of time and money are sunk into a project over and above expectations.

Here is an exercise to help you begin packaging your legal, consulting, accounting, tax, audit, financial, and non-attest services.

a) Imagine a Package of Services

Start by describing a complete package of services, including what problems it solves, its purpose, its features, its value, and its cost. In order to help you (and your clients) visualize the package service, we'll be using the term product to describe it. Exhibit 6-1, "Sample for Describing a Package of Services," is a form to help you with this step.

b) Examine Your Existing Services

Now that you've had the experience of productizing an intangible service, you take a look at all or most of the services your firm offers as a step toward making them more tangible.

In this exercise, you will list the products your firm offers. Exhibit 6-2, "Sample Form for Listing Firm Products," is a form to help compile this list.

c) Identify Client Purchases and Potential Purchases

The purpose of this exercise is to have you begin targeting clients to whom you can market additional products. In this exercise, select a client with whom you have a good working relationship—someone who likes you.

Exhibit 6-3, "Sample Form for Listing Current and Potential Sales," helps you list the products your client now buys from the firm and the products they should be buying.

d) List Actions Needed to Sell Potential Purchases

Consider and list what you must do to sell more. Exhibit 6-4, "Sample Form for Listing Actions Needed to Sell Additional Products," is a form for listing the marketing actions needed.

Okay, what did you learn from the exercises in steps a to d?

WHEN TESTED, MOST OF OUR CLIENTS AND STUDENTS FIND:

- They didn't realize all the services that the firm offers or that they themselves, were capable of offering.

- They didn't recognize that they had clients who should be buying many more services from their firm.

Hopefully, you now feel an urgency to sit down, away from the client's office and distractions (over lunch is best) and discuss with the client the possibility of having you fill these service needs, wants, and desires.

STEP #3. PRESCRIBE NOW–OPERATE LATER

Hopefully, you have more than your hands full. But, do what the Best Business Generators do: They market and sell when they are busy and schedule the additional work to be performed afterwards.

Why It Is Imperative To Market When You Are Busiest

There are six good reasons why busy times are the best time to market. They are:

Reason #1: You Have Much More Contact With Clients. Busy times are akin to Christmastime in the retail industry. There is never more opportunity to market your wares.

But what would happen to your retail clients if the salespeople hid in the back room during Christmas season? Or the merchandise wasn't put out for the customer to buy?

That's exactly what happens to attorneys when they are busy: They sell much less than they should. Attorneys go into a veritable seclusion from potential business when busy, because they are so preoccupied with getting the work out. (Don't draw the wrong conclusion, however; you have to get good, quality, timely work out during busy times too.) The point is that the great majority of our peers turn their minds off to new business during this time when they should have the exact opposite attitude.

We all know that you and your staff will encounter more clients (and prospective clients, if you do it right) during your busy times than any other. Great!

Remember our marketing definition:

> *Marketing is anything that puts you in front of someone you want to do business with. Doing work with clients is MARKETING.*

For instance, how often do we get to sit down with your clients, except for when you were working together? Every single client you have in your firm is a potential buyer for some other service or follow-on work. Every single client you have is a potential referral source, too. Don't ever forget that, or overlook this built-in marketing opportunity you have.

Reason #2: Clients Are In A State of Trauma. If your tooth hurts, you're going to take action, right? If your car has problems, you're going to get it fixed immediately, correct? If their taxes hurt, people are more likely to take action too. After all, who likes paying taxes?

> *Marketing Truth. Trauma is wonderful for marketing purposes because the more people hurt or ache about something, the more likely they are to take action.*

For example, perhaps in the past you've tried to have conversations with some of your clients about tax planning, estate planning, financial planning, or setting up wills and trusts. Usually, if attorneys attempt to discuss these topics with clients at all, they do it during slower time of the year, after the trauma of an engagement has gone away, thereby lessening the likelihood of people taking action or being interested in the topic.

Same analogy applies to dentistry. If your toothache goes away, do you want to talk to your dentist about having a root canal?

Therefore, begin discussion with your clients on legal implications, follow-on work and additional services when the trauma is fresh.

Set an appointment, right then and there, to meet after the current work is concluded to move forward.

The Best Business Generators have a saying: Prescribe now–operate later. That's how they create additional business after the current case. They strike while the iron is hot.

If you wait until after the case is over to discuss with your client how you might help them to improve their cash flow, prevent problems or reduce their legal exposure *it might be too late.*

The ache or hurt of the recent past dissipates into the challenge of the future as time passes.

Follow the lead of the Best Business Generators. Take advantage of the marketing opportunities that the current case provides and have these discussions with your clients now, while they have an interest.

Reason #3: Referral Sources Know About Client Trauma. Your referral sources are often in touch with your mutual clients during the case or engagement.

You need to have more contact with them, too, at this time of year for more referrals than ever before. You need to be in front of your referral sources more during the live engagement to get all of the referrals you deserve from them. "Out of sight, out of mind" applies here, too.

Reason #4: Attorneys Are "Heroes" During The Engagement. Those of you who go to social functions with clients that you are currently working with know exactly what we mean. During the rest of the year, if out socializing, people will often respond with a "ho-hum" when you tell them you're an attorney.

During a case, you're a hero! People want to talk to you! This is very good for marketing and building a practice. Take advantage of it. You are a popular person and have an opportunity to show yourself off to a lot of people who are in the trauma of the work. We know you're too tired to socialize when you are busiest. Catch up on your sleep later. We're talking about boosting your practice, here!

Reason #5: Nobody Else Is Even Thinking About It. Maybe the best reason to market, make contacts, and go places when you are busy is that your competition isn't even remotely thinking about it. That's right, there's a window of opportunity to do personal marketing in a virtual vacuum.

Take advantage of this marketing "monopoly" before the window closes.

We've had clients increase their practice 20 percent and more (and these aren't small practices, either) during the rest of the year by following the suggestions in this chapter and marketing during busy times.

When Do You Have Time to Do Marketing?

The Best Business Generators in the profession are always marketing and always thinking about business, even while they're grinding out the work.

They use those times during the day that are available to them to make more contact.

Most attorneys still eat lunch when busy, some even breakfast. Where do they eat? Usually at their desk, in the office, or with fellow co-workers.

Set aside two to three lunches a week, especially when you are busy, to make more contact with clients, former clients and people you should be doing more business with. Meet for breakfast or do whatever is most convenient for you.

We know, we know—you don't have time. So take a look at exactly what you're doing. Maybe you can delegate a bit of it, to free yourself up to "romance" your clients and find new ways to serve them.

What Will People Say?

What will people say if you call them or meet them for lunch? "Aren't you guys busy?"

To which you should reply, "Yes! Thank goodness, business is very good. But I always make time for my clients to hear how things are going for them. And explore any urgent legal concerns that may be on their mind. And get their advice on how to grow my practice with other people in their company."

That's verbatim what one of the Best Business Generators in the legal profession says to her contacts and clients. She maintains that it sets up their meetings to be even more productive than they might otherwise be. And she knows she has no personal marketing competition during busy season.

A managing partner of one of America's most successful law firms said, "We consider one hour of personal marketing as valuable to the firm as five hours of chargeable work."

STEP #4. KEEP THE CLIENT HAPPY

The Best Business Generators realize that marketing and selling are a lot like courtship. And the relationship with your clients is a lot like marriage. Like the Best Business Generators, you should never let the romance die in your client relationships. How can you get closer to your clients? How can you stay on top of their critical personal and business concerns?

Moreover, the Best Business Generators recognize that it takes a lot of time and effort to fortify their relationships with clients. And, they have to guard against complacency because any laziness on their part may, ultimately, cost them their clients. We find that more clients are lost due to poor communication and inattention than for any other reason.

Marketing Truth: Your best client is your competitor's best prospective client.

Keep this marketing truth in mind. Believe us, your clients are being actively courted. And losing one of your top clients is really painful and it will be difficult, expensive, and time-consuming to replace.

HERE ARE A FEW WAYS TO GUARANTEE A STABLE OF DELIGHTED CLIENTS.

Act Like a Business Doctor

The Best Business Generators are always examining the business operations of their top clients to find ways to help. They keep close eye on what's disturbing their clients and seeing where it hurts. Is their pension plan out of whack? Are they facing special financing requirements?

The Best Business Generators want their clients to see them as a valued business adviser. That's why they are the most enthusiastic cross-marketers of services. For they find that the more services they provide, the more their clients see them as an adviser, and not solely as a limited technician.

Because of cross-marketing, these clients are less likely to go outside of the firm to others for services.

Give Your Clients Referrals

Do you keep your eyes and eyes open to send business your client's way? Many of us think we do, but what do our clients think? How much business have you actually referred your clients' way this past year? Do you make a habit of sending your top clients some business or making introductions?

How do you do this? When you go to industry conferences, keep your eyes and ears open for new opportunities for your clients. Know the type of business that your clients are seeking. Be like the Best Business Generators; they enjoy finding business for their clients almost as much as they enjoy selling their own services.

Conduct Quarterly Meetings With Your Top Clients

To serve your clients as an adviser, you have to find out what's on their agenda. How do they plan to grow? What are their strategies? What problems are frustrating them most? Which areas require the most time and attention? What business problems are keeping them awake at night? In other words, stay on top of what's happening in their business. Use these quarterly meetings as a way of staying close to your clients.

We know an attorney who includes this type of meeting in all of her proposals, and she has dramatically increased her winning percentage accordingly. Because, in many cases, companies are switching from service providers who failed to communicate and stay in close regular contact with them.

Prospective clients don't want to engage a firm that would fail to listen to them. And, this attorney finds that the quarterly meetings provide tangible evidence of her distinctive commitment to listen and counsel.

Here's an example of how being in tune with your clients can lead to new opportunities.

An attorney noticed a trend in the industry he served—a trauma needing attention. He did the necessary research to familiarize himself with the applicable issues, then produced an executive briefing to reach out to clients, help resolve the trauma, and further promote his firm for new opportunities.

The executive briefing is a short (half hour) presentation of a leading-edge issue, or a source of severe trauma. It is not intended as a seminar or a deeply educational event. Instead, it's an executive summary that positions you as an expert and allows you to "sell" subtly.

Its best use is for cross-marketing a specialty service to a client. Or it can also be presented to an allied referral source for the same purpose. Use it with prospective clients too. It is a non-threatening way to move prospects off of neutral and marching toward becoming your client.

Here's an example of its use.

One of our clients served a number of mid-sized manufacturing companies. Many of these companies were either exporters or suppliers to big exporters. Consequently, many of them were feeling pressure to qualify for ISO 9000 certification to preserve their customer base.

Seeing this buyer trauma, the partner attended a series of intensive seminars on ISO 9000. Then, he contacted a local training firm in his city and purchased a fully scripted executive-level presentation titled "The Legal Ramifications of ISO 9000."

Next, he contacted his top 10 clients and made arrangements to conduct the executive briefing for them.

He fortified his relationships with his top clients and sustained his position as a business adviser in their eyes. Beyond client goodwill, he also was retained by six of these clients to help them assess their legal needs related to ISO 9000.

SUMMARY

- The Best Business Generators in the legal profession generate much of their new business by marketing additional services to their existing clients. They know that there is "gold in their own files."

- The only difference between marketing services to new clients and marketing new services to existing satisfied clients is that marketing to satisfied clients should be much easier.

- Existing, satisfied clients HAVE ALREADY MADE A DECISION TO DO BUSINESS WITH YOU which is the hardest hurdle to overcome in any sale.

- Rainmakers know that the more business they sell their existing clients, the more SECURE THE RELATIONSHIP IS.

  - As we said earlier, the purpose of marketing a tangible item is to sell it immediately. The purpose of marketing an intangible service is to provide the OPPORTUNITY.

- A success secret to MARKETING AN INTANGIBLE SERVICE IS TO MAKE IT AS TANGIBLE AS POSSIBLE.

- It's vital to "package" your services to successfully market them.

- Generate many more opportunities to sell by packaging your services into products, identifying which clients are in need of what, and then meeting with them to discuss their purchase of these "products."

EXERCISE 6-1

TARGETING A CLIENT

The purpose of this exercise is to have you begin targeting clients to market additional products to. In this exercise, select a client with whom you have a good working relationship—someone who likes you.

List below the products your client now buys from the firm and the products they should be buying:

Exhibit 6-1 Sample Form for Describing a Package of Services

Product description:

_____

_____

_____

Aches, hurts, problems, or desires this product solves:

1. _____

_____

2. _____

_____

3. _____

_____

4. _____

_____

5. _____

Product's purpose:

_____

_____

_____

_____

Product's features:

1. _____

_____

2. _____

_____

3. _____

_____

4. _____

_____

5. _____

_____

Purchase's value to the client:

1. _____

_____

2. _____

_____

3. _____

_____

4. _____

_____

5. _____

_____

Cost (range or fixed): $ _____

"Eye-catching" name of product (for example, the Protect Your Assets Program or the Estate Protection Plan):

Exhibit 6-2 Sample Form for Listing Firm Products

Product item:

1. _____

2. _____

3. _____

4. _____

5. _____

6. _____

7. _____

8. _____

9. _____

10. _____

11. _____

12. _____

Exhibit 6-3 Sample Form for Listing Current and Potential Sales

Missing Products Checklist

Client name: _____

Date:_____

List of products client is now buying:

1. _____

2. _____

3. _____

4. _____

5. _____

6. _____

7. _____

8. _____

9. _____

10. _____

List of products client should be buying:

Product 1: _____

Why should they buy? List three "hurts" you know of that this product will solve:

1. _____

_____

2. _____

_____

3. _____

_____

Contact person: _____

Cost (range): $ _____

Product 2: _____

Why should they buy? List three "hurts" you know of that this product will solve:

1. _____

_____

2. _____

_____

3. _____

_____

Contact person: _____

Cost (range): $ _____

Product 3: _____

Why should they buy? List three "hurts" you know of that this product will solve:

1. _____

_____

2. _____

_____

3. _____

_____

Contact person: _____

Cost (range): $ _____

Exhibit 6-4 Sample Form for Listing Actions Needed to Sell Additional Products

ACTION STEPS TO SELL THE ADDITIONAL PRODUCTS:

1. _____

   _____

   _____

   _____

2. _____

   _____

   _____

   _____

3. _____

   _____

   _____

   _____

4. _____

   _____

   _____

   _____

5. _____

   _____

   _____

WHAT DID YOU DISCOVER?

Okay—what did you learn from these exercises?

Most of our clients and students find:

They didn't realize all of the services the firm offers, or they, themselves, were capable of offering.

They didn't recognize that they had clients who should be buying many more services from their firm.

Hopefully, you now feel an urgency to sit down, away from the client's office and distractions (over lunch is best) and discuss with the client the possibility of having you fill these service needs, wants and desires.

Our job in this course is to provide you with the skills to generate and acquire many more quality contacts and leads, so you can add more (new and existing) profitable business to your practice. Through this exercise, we've done some of that. *Your job is to identify the clients with whom you have good relationships and repeat these exercises for them, and then meet with them.*

What are you waiting for?

CHAPTER 7

BUILDING POWERFUL MARKETING ALLIANCES

INTRODUCTION

Gaining the cooperation and committed help of closely allied referral sources is critical to building your practice.

Creating "allies" affects an external "sales force" for your practice—finding and introducing you to a steady stream of prospective clients.

As you've learned in our coverage of the Best Business Generators, the top business producers in the legal profession excel at building close, vital relationships with a *few potent allies.*

In this chapter we'll cover the strategies and tactics that will help you to accomplish this same objective.

First, we'll guide you through an audit of your current referral sources. Then, you'll learn a step-by-step process that will help you to maximize the quality of your referral relationships into *alliances.* As a final step, you'll prepare *a personal action plan* to get you started down the proper path with your allies.

WHY ARE ALLIANCES VITAL TO GROWING YOUR PRACTICE?

Except for marketing to your existing clients, building potent alliances is the most critical aspect of your personal marketing action plan. Why?

Well, growing your practice is a little bit like going to war—especially in the increasingly intensive competitive environment that all lawyers are facing. So, like nations entering a battle, you need allies on your side who are willing to commit to helping you win the war of practice development.

More to the point, the legal profession is truly a relationship business.

Your success is first and foremost dependent on the quality of your relationships —with clients AND allies. Therefore, your skills in managing your ally relationships can ultimately MAKE OR BREAK your practice.

THE POWER THAT ALLIANCES ADD TO YOUR PERSONAL MARKETING

Let's look at the power and advantages that allies bring to your business-building program.

Leverage. The first factor is LEVERAGE: Getting maximum impact and contribution from the effort, contacts and abilities of others. Let's face it: Given the time constraints, competing pressures, shifting critical priorities and various demands that you face, there is only so much that you can do yourself.

So, what can you do? Model what Best Business Generators do. *DELEGATE some of your practice development to your allies.* In effect, they become an outside sales force for you—finding a steady stream of prospects and contacts that would be valuable to you.

Word-of-Mouth Advertising. The second advantage for you is "WORD-OF-MOUTH" ADVERTISING: Recommendations from a respected attorney or banker carry a lot of weight. Frankly, prospective clients don't want to spend a lot of time researching law firms or making "cold" inquiries. So, they look to other advisers to get their recommendations for a service provider.

Solid allies will always be looking to bring your name up in the course of their significant business conversations. They know you, trust you and like you—and they expect that you'll be reciprocating in their behalf—looking for opportunities to bring business their way as well.

Complementary Strength. The third advantage is *COMPLEMENTARY STRENGTH* and collective impact. This means the mutual advantages that you and your ally bring TOGETHER is of greater value than what you have individually.

For example, your clients benefit from your close working relationship with an ally as you each bring expertise AND a working style that speeds communication and streamlines the process. Similarly, in marketing, each of you carries different advantages in terms of client bases, specialization and manpower.

Additionally, you'll be able to invest more time, money and support resources TOGETHER than either of you could invest SEPARATELY. Done correctly, this will translate into better, higher-impact marketing programs.

Mastermind. The final ingredient is the MASTERMIND effect. At times, business development can be a grueling, frustrating process. Also, on occasion you need to bounce ideas off of another entrepreneur who knows how you think, and can appreciate and understand your point of view, as well as the hurdles that you may be facing.

Allies become a support group.

They can become your "informal" business development advisors. Since they know you and understand your practice, their advice will be reasoned and pointed. In effect, they become your "MASTERMIND" group—providing the insight and support that we all need at times to succeed.

THE ALLIANCES THAT THE BEST BUSINESS GENERATORS ENJOY

In our study of the best business generators, the power of their alliances was a clear-cut component in their success. Without exception, they all confirmed that alliances were instrumental to their prosperity.

However, one fact did surprise us. We thought that these business generators would enjoy a wide network of "referral sources." Wouldn't it makes sense that they would have dozens of referral sources who passed them a lead or two based on their experience, reputation and personal charisma?

That wasn't the case. Instead, while they did gain referrals from their network, the MOST IMPORTANT source of high quality leads and new business originated from a FEW, STRONG AND ENDURING ALLIANCES. In fact, the bulk of their new business came from a *predictable stream of referrals from their best allies.* And, on average, the *quality of these referrals was exceptional*—each "lead" had a high probability of immediate closure for new business.

Here are a few typical examples of the power of allies from our training and consulting clients:

Firm in Ohio: The top business generator at this firm is a highly personable, senior partner. To give you an idea of his impact, this one person brings in 40% of the new clients to his firm with a partnership group of twenty partners. His passion is golf. Consequently, he's worked mostly with allies that share his interests, including golf.

By virtue of being "sporting types," as he put it, one year they decided to have a "referral" contest and keep score. Their goal was to go "all out" and find as many referrals for each other as possible over the following six months. From this group of four allies (a foursome is required for golf), each ally added new clients that amounted to 10–20% of their individual practices.

Leading Independent Firm in the Midwest: The bulk of this firm's work comes from the real estate and construction business. And the managing partner traditionally generates over 40% of their business ($20 million + in fees).

The majority of this work is generated from a tight-knit group of people who have known each other from their fraternity days at college. All became successful and remained friends. So, our client finds ways to remain close to this group. In fact, he keeps a chart with their names in a prominent area in his office. Each day, he looks at that chart to determine if there is anything he can do for those important allies. He finds any way to stay close, whether it's jogging with one or helping out another's important charitable cause.

Top Firm in Suburban Chicago: Another managing partner we work with built his firm from scratch to a $32 million practice.

As his firm grew, he recognized that the vast majority of his new business came from his banking allies. But, as his firm expanded and diversified, he found that his marketing program strayed away from his most important allies. Rather than mutually marketing with allies, he was stressing direct marketing to new clients, *without* outstanding success.

So, he re-oriented his firm's marketing effort. Recognizing the legacy of his firm and the importance of his confederates, he invested over 50% of his marketing effort into his allies and lavished attention on them. He joined in on their chamber of commerce leadership programs. Custom-tailored courses were offered to commercial loan officers—free of charge. All referrals were directed to the allies who brought in referrals. What was the effect? Despite an economic downturn at the time, this firm experienced double-digit growth in fees.

The way we look at the power of ally relationships is this: *an ally is basically a partner in building your business.* But you can't deal with them as you would a partner! You must treat them like your most important client. Think about the relationship in these terms: Initially, you "SOLD" this person on being your ally. This "SALE" has led to a number of new sales (OR REPEAT BUSINESS). Isn't this similar to the relationship you have with your clients to a degree?

THE CRITICAL DIFFERENCES BETWEEN REFERRAL NETWORKING AND ALLIANCES

ALLIANCES VS REFERRALS

ALLIANCES	REFERRALS
ONE OF YOUR TOP 3 SOURCES OF REFERRALS	GIVES YOU A FEW LEADS OVER TIME
PRE-SELLS YOU TO OTHERS	SUBMITS YOUR NAME
HAS A PERSONAL STAKE IN YOUR SUCCESS AND SHOWS STRONG COMMITMENT	NOT AS CLOSE OF A WORKING RELATIONSHIP–OFFERS YOU AND OTHERS
MUTUALLY BENEFICIAL	MAY NOT BE BALANCED
STRONG PERSONAL CHEMISTRY	CORDIALITY
HIGHLY ENTREPRENEURIAL AND MARKETING ORIENTED	NOT AN INTENSIVE COOPERATIVE MARKETING EFFORT

Please recognize that there is an important distinction between managing your alliances and building your referral network. (We'll cover the keys to successful networking in Chapter 9).

HERE ARE THE KEY ATTRIBUTES OF AN ALLIANCE:

Generates a Significant Number of High Quality Leads: An ally is somebody who finds you a lot of leads —somebody who is absolutely instrumental in building your practice. By contrast, a "referral source" may generate a lead or two once in a while.

Will Act as Your Salesperson: Allies are adept at "pre-selling" your services. They know you and your practice well enough to qualify prospects on their need, want or desire for your service.

Demonstrates Strong Commitment: An ally is somebody who has a personal stake in your success. In most cases, it's a long-standing relationship. In fact, you may be the attorney that he or she sends ALL of her clients and contacts to see. You may be the only person who jointly markets services with her firm.

The closure ratio is much higher for leads generated by allies than by "referral sources" who are often weakly submitting your name along with others.

Is a Mutually Beneficial Relationship: No enduring ally relationship can be wholly one-sided. Therefore, vital alliances are highly balanced. For example, you trade business back & forth. You counsel one another on business development or technical issues. You trust your ally to serve your clients, friends and contacts, and vice versa. Perhaps, you share mutual marketing investments. And you may invest a lot of time communicating to stay on top of "your business together".

"Referral relationships" are often unbalanced and one-sided. Ever formally keep track of referrals received and owed? Allies make sure you get taken care of; referral sources tend to forget.

Is Marked by Solid Personal Rapport and Chemistry: An alliance is typically sparked by a good personal working relationship—and often develops into friendship. This is essential to its success as each of you probably have other options for referrals and alliances. So, there needs to be a "reason" for a continuing relationship—and this strong personal connection provides the foundation upon which the "business" relationship thrives.

Is "Entrepreneurial": We've found that both parties must have similar business building ambitions for the alliance to work effectively. An entrepreneur is always on the hunt for ways to grow, therefore, he or she respects and seeks allies who share this goal.

Unfortunately, many attorneys often waste their precious referrals by giving them to colleagues who have little or no interest or competence in building their own practices, when these referrals could have been invested in people who do (and would reciprocate as an ally).

A FOUR-STEP PROCESS TO MANAGING YOUR ALLIANCES

Now you can see why there's no question that alliances are critical to growing your business, and you understand the qualities that lead to a productive alliance.

Let's look at how you can create or enhance an ally relationship. For the rest of this chapter, we'll show you proven methods and techniques for managing and improving these relationships.

HERE'S OUR FOUR-STEP APPROACH TO BUILDING YOUR ALLIANCES:

STEP #1: AUDIT YOUR ALLIANCES.

Appraise the QUANTITY of leads and new business that you trade back and forth. Then, evaluate the QUALITY of the relationship—in terms of personal chemistry, compatibility, entrepreneurial ability and other important intangibles.

STEP #2: FOCUS ON A TOP FEW.

Next, concentrate on your top three or four relationships intently. Review your list to pick those allies who will be most important to your future success.

STEP #3: AGREE ON AN UP-FRONT CONTRACT.

Formalize the goals for your alliance. Define your mutual "conditions of relationship satisfaction." Consider the objectives of your ally. Balance your viewpoints and define the precise, shared goals for your alliance.

STEP #4: DEVELOP AN ALLIED MARKETING PLAN.

The final step is to come up with your mutual plan of attack. This is your "working agreement." And, later in this chapter, we'll show you some of the better-allied marketing ideas we've encountered and created—the proven winners.

NOW YOU CAN GET STARTED:

STEP #1: HOW TO AUDIT THE QUALITY OF YOUR CURRENT ALLIANCES

Let's take a closer look at your alliances. Use the following form to complete these exercises:

Exhibit 7-1: Auditing the Quality of Your Ally Relationships Brainstorming Worksheet

	What I Received Last Year			What I Gave Out Last Year	
Name of Ally	# of Leads	$ in Fees		# of Leads	$ in Fees
1.					
2.					
3.					
4.					
5.					
6.					
7.					
8.					
9.					
10.					
11.					
12.					

STEP #1A: RANK ORDER YOUR KEY ALLIANCES

Begin with your best one: the banker, lawyer or colleague who is the MOST Important asset in growing your practice. Then, list the SECOND best ally—and so on. Continue on until you run out of allies worth mentioning.

STEP #1B: REVIEW THE LAST YEAR

Think about how many leads this person provided to you. Then, identify the amount of fees that were generated by the new clients from these leads. It's OK to estimate; you don't have to get the numbers exactly. Just make sure that they are reasonably accurate.

STEP #1C: LOOK AT THE RELATIONSHIP THROUGH THE EYES OF YOUR ALLIES

You're now going to re-do the same analysis, but through their eyes. How many leads did you provide to them? What estimated fee revenue did they generate from you?

STEP #1D: NOTE YOUR REACTIONS TO THIS LIST

What initial responses come to mind? Are there any surprises? Do the relationships seem balanced? Don't worry about any hard and fast conclusions right now. You'll confront those later as the auditing process continues.

STEP #2: FOCUSING ON YOUR TOP ALLIANCES

STEP #2A: FOCUS ON A FEW, HIGH PRIORITY RELATIONSHIPS

A major tenet of building alliances is to limit yourself to the number of relationships you can manage and invest in. So, for the purposes of this exercise, let's work with your top three allies. Now, we'll quickly audit these relationships a bit further.

STEP #2B: CAN THEY BRING YOU CLIENTS IN YOUR TARGET MARKET NICHES—YOUR IDEAL CLIENTS?

This may seem like an odd step. But, sometimes, your traditional allies may not be the best source for the type of clients that you want to attract TODAY and in the FUTURE. For example, you may want to emphasize a new service for business clients—instead of taking on a ton of individual tax clients. BUT, this DOES NOT mean that you forsake this ally. It simply means that other allies could move up higher in rank order if they are better positioned to bring you IDEAL clients.

STEP #2C: TAKE A LOOK AT THE INTANGIBLES

How is your personal chemistry with this ally?

Will they look forward to an even closer, more proactive working relationship?

Are they entrepreneurially oriented?

Would they be willing to aggressively market on a cooperative basis?

Now, think about your answers. Does this ally look like it will still be a top source of new business for you? Is there any significant reason to think that this relationship will decline or "dry up" this year?

If you think that these top three relationships will continue to thrive, proceed to the next step. If you see one of these relationships to be at risk, then pick another ally relationship to take through this process.

DON'T ELIMINATE A TOP-THREE ALLY RELATIONSHIP UNTIL YOU GO THROUGH THE NEXT STEP. Because this is a valuable ally, you want to make sure that you fully understand how you can make this relationship work best. Armed with the information you'll gather in Step #3, you can make an informed judgment on how to re-vitalize this relationship. Or you can decide to invest the bulk of your attention to three other relationships.

STEP #3: AGREEING ON AN UP-FRONT CONTRACT

STEP #3A: WHAT ARE YOUR "CONDITIONS OF RELATIONSHIP SATISFACTION" FOR THIS ASSOCIATION?

Specifically define what you need to yield from this working relationship to be delighted.

What are your objectives?

How many leads and referrals would be satisfactory?

What type of cooperation is required?

How is communication and follow-through currently working?

What has worked well in this relationship that you want to sustain?

Where is there room for improvement?

What specific measures and guidelines should be set to gauge how well this relationship is moving?

What type of joint marketing efforts do you want to attack?

What kind of introductions do you want from this ally?

Think through all these factors. Then, write down a set of specific goals. Make sure that these objectives are reasonable and achievable. To the extent possible, make these goals precise and quantifiable.

Review now what you have really accomplished with Step #3A. YOU'VE LAID THE GROUNDWORK NECESSARY TO MANAGE THIS RELATIONSHIP. The problem with alliances is that they are rarely formalized, contractual agreements. Because of the "loose" nature of these alliances, they tend not to be carefully managed. Using our approach, you take the initiative. Also, you've carefully defined your expectations—so that your ally can understand them and aim for your goals.

STEP #3B: WHAT ARE YOUR ALLY'S "CONDITIONS OF RELATIONSHIP SATISFACTION?"

You are only half finished with this step. REMEMBER THE BALANCE RULE. For an alliance to work there has to be strong mutual benefit. So, look at this working relationship through the eyes of your ally. Reconsider some of the same questions in Step #3A. But, answer them as your ALLY might.

> Specifically, how does your working relationship benefit this ally?
>
> How much business did you generate for him or her?
>
> What's working from his or her point of view?
>
> What would she change in your working relationship?
>
> What marketing programs would he beneficial to him or her?
>
> What introductions could you make for him or her?

STEP #3C: FORMALIZING YOUR UP-FRONT CONTRACT WITH YOUR ALLY

Now, it's time to agree on a "treaty" with your ally. We call this an "up-front contract."

Set up a meeting with your ally, preferably a relaxed lunch away from the distractions of the office—where the sole purpose is to discuss how you can best work together for the upcoming year.

Start by stating your purpose for the meeting.

Then, review your conditions of relationship satisfaction—giving your ally a precise understanding of your goals for the working relationship.

Tell him or her the quantified objectives that you aspire to—in terms of number of leads and introductions, cooperative marketing as well as any enhancements you seek in the alliance.

Then, get their reaction. Are your goals reasonable? Are they attainable? Are these priorities that they can commit to? What doesn't make sense from their standpoint?

Now, ask your ally for their conditions of relationship satisfaction.

> Do they dovetail with your goals and objectives?
>
> What can you specifically agree to in terms of mutual goals for referrals and introductions?
>
> What will be your plan of attack for working together?

What corrective improvements do they desire in your working relationships?

How often will you meet to keep things on track?

Come to a meeting of the minds. Document what you agreed to in the meeting.

Here's what you have accomplished: You now have clear, shared goals. Also, you have "formalized" your working relationship with your ally—you defined the precise ways that you can help each other best. Beyond these advantages, you also have brainstormed on the kind of cooperative marketing actions that can benefit both of you.

STEP #4: DEVELOP YOUR COOPERATIVE MARKETING PLAN OF ATTACK

In this step you will develop a precise plan for mutual marketing. While you may have some initial ideas—or you may have some programs that have worked well historically—take a look at the ideas we summarize in this section.

You'll see our list of the top eleven proven winners for allied marketing programs. Then, look if you can select the best fit for your practice. And, incorporate them into your plan of attack.

But, before we get started, we have to review our cardinal rule of marketing. If you get just one thing out of this course, remember this critical marketing principle: *"Marketing is a contact sport."* This means that the best form of marketing is that which puts you in direct (preferably face-to-face) contact with your best clients and ideal, qualified prospects.

All of your other marketing can only complement your direct marketing efforts. But, contact-making marketing should always be your highest priority.

Review the following contact-making, allied marketing programs that have proven to be winners for our clients and students.

PROVEN MARKETING PROGRAMS

Program #1: Shared Client Meetings

If you both serve the same clients, this is the place to start.

If a legal or consulting ally serves a client of yours, then coordinate your approach to service. Utilize a quarterly or semi-annually "How's Business?" program. If you both serve the same clients, this is the place to start.

Get your ally and the lead executives of your client together in a relaxed atmosphere over lunch or in a conference room, preferably away from the distractions of their office.

Then, ask the client's owner, CEO or CFO to bring you up to date on the significant developments in their business. Your role is to simply listen and advise—you're not there to sell. Get them to review their significant goals and objectives for the upcoming quarter or six months. Offer up questions, issues and concerns.

What do you accomplish with this? First, you both reinforce your position as trusted business advisors. Second, you provide a higher level of service because you are both fully up to speed on your client's critical business concerns. And, you speed communication and streamline coordination with your ally in serving this client.

Simultaneously, you and your ally strengthen the relationship with your client. And, guess what? Somehow, you will generate additional business. You will likely find direct "aches, hurts, problems, needs, wants or desires" that you can remedy. Or you'll walk out with mutual and/or individual referrals—based on this close contact that amazingly few other attorneys even think of offering.

Whether you charge for meetings like this with your best clients is up to you. We believe that meetings like this are, indeed, marketing in its truest, and most valuable, sense. Some of our clients charge for these meetings, most don't. Invest your marketing time and dollars where there is the highest potential for payoff: with your best clients, best potential clients and allies.

These meetings are an added value that will help you secure many more "best clients" than the typical attorney who certainly doesn't offer this kind of client service.

Program #2: Make Direct Introductions to Clients and Prospects

This is the obvious next priority.

Often, we hear from professionals who haven't received many new referrals lately from their referral sources. The referral sources explain it away saying that they haven't brought in many new clients or customers recently. Sound familiar?

Then, now's the time that each of you should take a fresh look at your clients and prospects.

Something may have changed or developed within your client base that might be an opportunity for your ally. If you both take the time to diagnose carefully and individually each client, you have to find some high closure possibilities that you and your ally can capitalize on immediately.

Jake, a client of ours, recently audited his own client base with an eye for possibility for his close ally, Jeff, a CPA in general practice. He discovered that over thirty of his clients needed consulting work done, eight were in need of a financial expert witness, twenty-two needed fresh wills, trusts and estate work, thirty needed business valuations, six were starting new businesses, and three had been actively looking to replace their existing CPA firm. This was just for starters. He started feeding this work to Jeff incrementally.

Jeff, faced with an avalanche of new business, immediately contacted twenty of his best clients to see if they were displeased with their current attorney and made personal introductions to Jake to sixteen of them, fourteen of whom hired Jake immediately for corporate or individual work.

Note: Jake, being the effective service provider that he is, has been keeping close track of the number of new clients Jeff owes him.

Program #3: Start a "Bring a Client to Lunch Club"

Contact your allies and begin a "bring a client to lunch club." Each month trade off the responsibility of bringing one client to a mutual, low-key, luncheon with your referral ally.

To stay in control, you keep score.

Under what pretense? None. It just makes good business sense to introduce your clients to CPAs, insurance people, etc. that they might have use for in the future.

Having done so, this is another person-to-person contact with your client and shows you care about their welfare. In inviting your client, merely state that you'd like them to meet someone you think highly of. Why wouldn't they come? If they're not interested, go on to another client.

One of our clients in an area of the country where business is slow took our suggestion on this one. Within only two months, he had generated over $180,000 in new billings because of these direct introductions, resulting in new clients and referrals.

Program #4: Trade Marketing and Sales Materials

Earlier, we talked about how your allies are basically an external sales force for your practice. So, go the extra mile. Make sure that you have materials from your ally that can make it easier to "sell" her to a prospect or client—and vice versa. Give your ally some of your key materials as well.

At a minimum, maintain an accessible inventory of each other's business cards. Better yet, keep some of their basic brochures and contact information available. Best of all, ensure that you know the service specialties and industry niches where your ally and you excel. Then, secure access to each other's specialized marketing materials.

Why is this important? We've found that this simple step strengthens the impact of your cross-selling activities—because it streamlines the follow-through process. Think about it. If your ally meets a prospect for you and passes along your card or a brochure—then the prospect is ready for your call. Moreover, the strength of the recommendation to the prospect is even greater than normal because your ally went the extra mile and followed up aggressively. They gave the prospect everything necessary to either call you —or be ready and informed when you call.

Program #5: Executive Briefings

Let's say that both you and your ally have targeted specific, related service specialties. Then consider executive briefings as your next mutual marketing project.

An executive briefing is a personalized presentation on an important topic. It is not a "sales call." Its purpose is informative in nature, and low key.

In doing an executive briefing you could focus on a specific industry's key issues—such as wholesale distributors and the hot issues that are facing their industry at this particular time. Or you could go cross-industry and concentrate on a crucial business "hurt, ache or trauma"—such as estate planning or business succession issues that can effect everyone.

Then, what's the best way to promote your service offering? Put on a seminar? Do an advertisement?

NO. Where you should ALWAYS start in marketing: with your mutual base of existing clients.

Simply develop a BRIEF (30–45 minute maximum) mutual presentation on the pain and pitfalls that business owners, executives or individuals face in the particular situation you have selected to discuss. Then, highlight the clients with the highest need for this service offering. Schedule a series of individual meetings with these clients at your place of business or theirs (in a conference room).

Here's what to do at these meetings: Start by setting the ground rules. Your goal is to get as much interaction with the client's executives as possible. You want to ask the clients questions and react to how these circumstances are impacting their business so that you can qualify them for your services. Then, you make your presentation. Afterwards, have a discussion on how your client is struggling with these related issues.

Needless to say, if your client sees an urgent need to address this service—then follow through appropriately.

Next, go beyond your existing clients. Do you have any target clients who would benefit from this presentation? If so, go for it. Can you get a referral into an ideal prospective client? Then, use this as an entree —an excuse to get together.

Keep working this approach. It's a great weapon to have in your arsenal.

Program #6: Joint Speaking Engagements

You now have a presentation that's been tested with your existing clients. Moreover, you've heard and seen their reactions.

You have a wealth of information on how these problems and challenges impact their business or personal success. In other words, you have something valuable to offer. What do you do next?

Find more ideal prospects and make this same presentation. Target associations or organizations where your ideal prospects gather. Then, find out if you have a client or contact that can refer you into this organization as a speaker. Or, get them to introduce you to the president or program chairman—and sell your presentation ideas to this group.

Follow the methods we cover in our chapter on public speaking to turn speaking engagements into hot leads.

Program #7: Breakfast Roundtables and Special Interest Groups

Once again, let's say that you have a mutually important, targeted service area. Hopefully, it can be the same area that you targeted in programs 5 and 6 above. Instead of doing a presentation, try a breakfast roundtable of six to eight participants. In these roundtables, you act as moderator or facilitator. Your goal is to spur a group discussion on trends or critical "aches or hurts" that this group is facing.

These roundtables should be with a "peer group." You invite the ideal prospects that fit the service profile.

Once you've identified your target service and priority "peer group," how do you get people to attend? First, INVITE YOUR CLIENTS who fit the profile. Why? Because they may need the service. Also, they will act as your "salesperson" in the roundtable—testifying to the quality of your service and value that you add to their business.

Then, both you and your ally should ASK THE CLIENTS WHO ARE ATTENDING TO INVITE ONE OTHER PERSON WHO FITS THE PROFILE. In this way, your client acts as your sponsor. And, it's easy for them to access and persuade a peer to attend, as there is no selfish reason for them personally to invite a prospective client. Therefore, prospects are more likely to attend. Also, it makes the session more appealing to a prospect, and it appears more valuable, if a trusted peer makes the invitation—instead of a stranger like you.

What if you need more people to attend? Or what if you want to run multiple sessions? You've got two options. First, find other contacts who can bring in prospects that fit the profile. Perhaps target the head of an association—or some other contacts that are highly networked. Or get others in your firm to invite a prospect or one of their clients or referral sources.

Here's your second option. Believe it or not, our clients have had luck in sending out "cold" invitations to prospects for roundtable discussions. But, there are a few secrets to making this work correctly.

First, use personal stationary or "invitation" stock—like wedding invitations. Everybody tends to pay much more attention to invitations, so it's more likely to reach your target. Second, mention other individuals who will be attending so that they see that their peers will be there. Finally, mail them out in groups of 25 or so, then make a follow up call to see if you can get them to attend.

How do you prepare and conduct the roundtable? Simply prepare an outline. Then, ask each person to introduce him or herself. After introductions, ask directed questions and get the participants talking. Make sure that you draw in all of the attendees so that they feel comfortable, even if you have to call on some who are more reserved.

After a few minutes, you'll find that the conversation takes off on its own! You just have to keep it flowing. Keep it on schedule and adjourn on time.

Two last points on these breakfast roundtables: Make sure you take notes on the problems and "aches" that surfaced during the discussion. You can then make use of these ideas as a way to follow through with the participants to see if they want to set an appointment, and as a next step, in a direct mail piece.

Also, make sure that you send a hand-written thank you note on your personal stationary. *** This adds the critical personal touch that makes an impact.***

Program #8: Joint Case Studies and Mailings

How can you make use of the feedback and information that you generated through the executive briefings (Program #5) or the breakfast roundtables (Program #7)?

Simply write a brief article (one page front and back). Keep it on an "executive summary" level. Include as many quotes and as much feedback from participants as possible.

Review Chapter 11 on writing high-powered direct marketing material that sells.

Program #9: Joint Seminars

Based on the last few steps, you and your ally have a winning presentation. Moreover, you received some solid feedback and client experiences that add flavor and potency to your presentation.

Now you have an option: You might want to put on a seminar. But, make sure that there is a broad enough audience to warrant a seminar.

Who is the target attendee? Is there a target association that would see this as a valuable seminar to sponsor? Can you get the right people to attend?

Putting on seminars takes planning and skill, but there are a few key concepts we want to cover here.

We have a rule of thumb regarding conducting seminars: ALWAYS GET AN ORGANIZATION TO SPONSOR YOUR SEMINAR. ONLY PUT IT ON BY YOURSELF AS A LAST RESORT.

Why is this smart? First, organizations are in the seminar business—they do it all of the time, while this is a SIDELINE business for you. Second, the associations are "in-tune" with their members' key concerns and educational requirements. And they can handle all the little details that can make a seminar successful (and be very time consuming). Finally, being sponsored lends credibility to you and the topic that you just can't replace in getting people to attend.

PUTTING ON SEMINARS BY YOURSELF IS DIFFICULT UNLESS IT'S PREDOMINANTLY AIMED AT CLIENTS. AND, EVEN THEN, IT'S TOUGH TO GET GOOD ATTENDANCE.

The reason we caution you is that self-sponsored seminars can be an awful waste of time, money and effort. They're tough to pull off properly. The self-sponsored seminar in your town may be over-saturated.

We suggest you explore the earlier steps of joint marketing initially, specifically executive briefings, breakfast roundtables and speaking engagements. Then, you'll KNOW how compelling a seminar might be.

Otherwise, unless you handle it right, the cost and risk of putting on a seminar can be substantial—and the payback tenuous.

Program #10: Jointly Sponsored Special Events

Special event marketing is one of the fastest growing fields in the art of promotion.

It is also a tool that any practitioner can employ. If you're with a sizeable firm, you could consider a major event, like sponsoring a tent at a sporting event or endorsing a major charitable event. Next time you see an important golfing tournament, for example, look at all the corporate sponsors who bring their top customers to the course.

But, even if you're a smaller firm or sole practitioner, you can do the same thing on a smaller scale. Whether it's a local township fair, school/fraternity alumni event, a college concert or a church event, there's often a chance for sponsorship. Also, special meetings, guest speakers and/or hospitality suites for major association meetings are a natural for any size firm.

Special event marketing is within the reach of most firms. And, explore why special event marketing is so hot: it can be highly productive and allows for lots of face-to-face contact.

SPECIAL EVENT MARKETING GIVES YOU THE PERFECT EXCUSE TO PERSONALLY GREET EVERY GUEST AND PARTICIPANT AT THE EVENT, BECAUSE YOU ARE THE HOST.

Firstly, you might not get warm, personal one-on-one contacts like this too often. It's a marvelous opportunity.

Secondly, today there's a lot of marketing "clutter" competing for the attention of your clients and prospects. Events stick out amongst the clutter as in many cases, it is an "EVENT" in every sense of the word. Done correctly, it is a special attraction and something unusual.

And thirdly, it allows you to make "special invitations." Your clients and prospects will be flattered that you thought of them—even if they can't make it.

So, put your head together with your ally to see where you have some mutual interests, along with organizations that might have some sponsorship possibilities.

As you think through some options, here are some rules of thumb: Make sure that it is a "lure" to the type of people that you want to attract. And it has to "live up" to your professional standards. Avoid anything that could offend or upset your clients.

Make sure it fits into your cooperative marketing budget with this particular ally—in terms of both money and time. If, for example, your ally can't find enough time to properly "work the event," consider someone else to go in with.

Don't sponsor too many events. Pick one or two at most a year. Then, concentrate your time and money on these—so that there is a higher impact.

Once you pick the event, you and your ally should put your full effort into getting your clients and mutually ideal prospects to attend. Print up the invitations with an RSVP return card. Send them out. And follow up with a call to inspire them to attend.

Prepare to market and sell at the event. We'll cover some of the principles of contact making later.

But, here are a few additional ideas:

- *Have a ready supply of sales collateral and promotional material at the event. Keep this material in an area where people will bump into it and pick it up.*

- *Get your allies and colleagues to the event. This boosts the attendance.* You also will want them to proactively "work the room."

- *Go to the event with a plan. After all, you're there to either sell or to build relationships.* Keep this in mind.

- *Bring your calendar or PDA so that you can book appointments with any interested parties.*

After the event, *follow up.* Send personal notes and make calls as warranted.

Special event marketing can be a potent weapon. And, it works best when you "team up" with an ally. Consequently, keep an eye open for opportunities that make sense for both of you.

Program #11: Double-team Associations and Social Organizations

Here's our final suggestion for allied, cooperative marketing. Again, its main purpose is to coordinate your promotional strategy and agree on a plan of attack. In this way, you amplify your success.

We suggest that you and your ally "double-team" the associations that your best clients and most attractive prospects frequent. Come up with a clear scheme to position both of you visibly within the organization.

Target different leadership positions with your ally. One could aim for being president, while the other should go after the program chairmanship.

Get your clients involved in leadership positions, too, so you can have "inside salespeople" infecting the organization on your behalf. Then influence others in your firm to be active —in terms of both attending and taking leadership positions. This will multiply your word of mouth marketing within the group and gain greater "market share" for the firm within the organization.

Seek ways to showcase your expertise in the operations of the organization. Develop a business plan for the organization. Review the accounting and financial procedures. How could you improve the productivity of the operations? Take a look at the accounting systems and software. Make a tangible show of your expertise.

Maintain a visible position in the programs of the organization. Make sure that either you, your ally or your clients are frequent speakers—or ensure that you are in the position to introduce speakers at events.

Seek feedback from members on their satisfaction with the organization's membership. Sponsor informal breakfasts or lunch "brainstorming" sessions to find ways to make the organization as valuable as possible. Or, sponsor a "member" satisfaction survey.

Why does this make sense? It shows your commitment to client service and satisfaction. Isn't that a great way for your firm to be perceived?

These ideas are just a start. Think through EVERY way you can promote yourself cooperatively with your ally. After all, you'll be investing a lot of time and energy in this organization. So, find ways to make the most of your involvement.

A LESSON FROM THE BEST BUSINESS GENERATORS: CASE EXAMPLE OF AN ALLIANCE

Why have we spent so much time on the importance of alliances? That's easy. It's a proven application of resources that leads to marketing success and one that the best business generators routinely employ. All we've done is to systematize and formalize this practice. Let's take a look at the power of the up-front contract.

One of our clients is the managing partner of a law firm on the west coast. He felt that his firm's business generation was flat. At our request he conducted an "audit" of his firm's top alliances—using the same process we've just reviewed. One fact jumped out at him.

The top law firm in his suburban area was traditionally a superb source of highly qualified referrals. But, for the past year, his firm had received NO referrals from this previously solid referral source. Upon further investigation, it turned out that his partners collectively sent at least ten clients to this firm over the same period of time.

However, each individual partner sent one or two referrals to a variety of individual partners, and no one knew what the others were doing. Thus, the total benefit of these leads to the firm was not obvious. In addition, the managing partner realized that he hadn't stayed in close contact with his counterpart at the firm.

Initially, the managing partner called together a few of his partners to brainstorm on how they could market cooperatively with this firm. Then, they set to paper their conditions of relationship satisfaction—as well as their plan of attack to pursue the marketing programs they targeted. Next, the managing partner called up the other managing partner to set up a "working lunch" to explore ways that they "help each other's business to grow."

They met in a conference room at the law firm—just the managing partner and his peer.

Our client thanked the managing partner for getting together. He said that he regretted that their working relationship was not as strong as it used to be. This caught the attorney by surprise. And, he was further startled by the fact that his firm had not referred any clients to this law firm as he always personally valued the referral relationship that they had built.

Then, they brainstormed on exploring ways to market together. They drew up their conditions of relationship satisfaction on a flip chart.

Here's the agreement they reached:

- *Goals: They agreed to trade at least 10 business leads back and forth for the upcoming year.*

- *Networking: The CPA was just named to be the president of the local chamber of commerce and he asked the managing partner to be on the board.*

- *Cooperative Marketing: They agreed to put together a joint presentation on estate and retirement planning—and they resolved to put on a series of joint seminars to both the bank's customers as well as the firm's clients. In addition, the accounting firm's PR department would aim to book joint speaking engagements at top associations.*

- *Training: The law firm would put on some breakfast training sessions for the construction/ real estate loan officers at the bank. These sessions were geared to help the attorneys understand the intricacies and complexities of recent regulatory developments with the accounting firm's clients.* In addition, this allowed the younger professionals (managers, staff and associates) to meet and build rapport.

- *Sales Materials: The bank often encounters entrepreneurial customers who are starting up their own businesses. And many of these customers lack legal advisors.* So, the law firm provided them with a "business-start up" kit with reference materials on the legal and regulatory issues that impact new businesses. All of this material was placed in a folder with the firm's name and contact information prominently displayed along with a business card of the managing partner.

- *Social Mixing: The accounting firm sponsored a "mixer" with the professional staff of the law firm. At the beginning of the get-together, the CPA managing partner reviewed their service capabilities and priorities for growing the firm.* The law firm partner did likewise. After the presentations, a guest speaker trained the total group on key networking skills. Then, the firms' professionals practiced their skills and networked with each other.

- *Quarterly Relationship Review Meetings: The CPA managing partner and the law firm managing partner agreed to meet on a quarterly basis. They vowed to keep in touch to make sure that the working relationship stayed vital.* Their personal secretaries were delegated the task of scheduling these meetings for them.

- *Referral Ledger Started:* **At the law firm managing partner's suggestion, the CPA and managing partner each began keeping a "referral ledger" at their businesses to account for referrals given and received to make sure the previous situation didn't re-occur. They designated their personal secretaries as the keeper of these books.**

What was the net effect of all of these efforts? Not only did the law firm realize its goal of 10 new business clients—they doubled it. And they built a foundation of commitment and consistency that will make this relationship vital and enduring.

CONCLUSION

Let's review what you learned in this chapter.

You now appreciate the practice building power of alliances and see how alliances augment and multiply the impact of your marketing efforts.

Don't settle for shallow relationships with your best allies. Instead, MANAGE your ally relationships. Make it a consistent, daily, high priority. And use the four-step management process we covered:

- *Audit your allied relationships*

- *Focus on your top allies intently*

- *Agree on a clear, up-front contract with your ally to clarify your shared*

   goals and objectives

- *Develop a cooperative marketing plan of attack that concentrates on the proven marketing winners—ones that put you in direct contact with your best clients and ideal prospects.*

Now you have built critical advantages into your practice building programs. You have leverage, word of mouth advertising, complementary and synergistic strength, and a mastermind group to support your marketing program.

Don't go it alone. Together with your allies, you'll amplify your success—and be a step ahead of your competitors who rely on less.

SUMMARY

- Gaining the cooperation and committed help of closely allied referral sources is critical to building your practice

- Creating "allies" affects an external "sales force" for your practice

- Allies give you leverage, word of mouth advertising, complementary and synergistic strength, and a mastermind group to support your marketing program.

- A four-step approach to building your alliances:

  Step #1: Audit Your Alliances

  Step #2: Focus on A Few

  Step #3: Agree on an Up-Front Contract

  Step #4: Develop an Allied Marketing Plan

- "Marketing is a contact sport." The best form of marketing is that which puts you in direct (preferably face-to-face) contact with your best clients and ideal, qualified prospects.

- Allied marketing programs that have proven to be winners:

  Program #1: Shared Client Meetings

  Program #2: Make Direct Introductions to Clients and Prospects

  Program #3: Start a "Bring-a-Client-to-Lunch Club"

  Program #4: Trade Marketing and Sales Materials

  Program #5: Executive Briefings

  Program #6: Joint Speaking Engagements

  Program #7: Breakfast Roundtables and Special Interest Groups

  Program #8: Joint Case Studies and Mailings

  Program #9: Joint Seminars

  Program #10: Jointly Sponsored Special Events

  Program #11: Double-Team Associations and Social Organizations

- Don't settle for shallow relationships with your best allies. Instead, MANAGE your ally relationships.

CHAPTER 8

A SYSTEMATIC APPROACH THAT GUARANTEES QUALITY REFERRALS

INTRODUCTION

As we've mentioned earlier, the Best Business Generators in the legal profession rely greatly on referrals from clients and allies to produce the majority of their new business.

Sadly, most attorneys just don't seem to get their share of referrals that would help their practices grow dramatically and profitably with the targeted clients they want. And if they do receive a referral, many simply don't follow through on it and it goes to waste!

By drawing on this vast resource of receiving referrals, you can, as the top producers do, *turn your clients and referral sources into your sales force!*

In this chapter we'll show you how to use a systematic approach that guarantees referrals because it has been proven by hundreds of our clients and students over the past twenty years.

WHY DON'T YOU GET MORE REFERRALS?

In 2003, we conducted a study of 200 clients of law firms, large and small, spread out over the US and Canada. We wanted to know if these clients gave their attorneys, how often and why not.

The results were quite interesting and not exactly as we expected:

- A full 50% of those interviewed said they had, indeed, given their service provider referrals

- Eighty percent of the other fifty percent (who did not give referrals) said they did not primarily because they had never been requested to give a referral, didn't know their lawyer wanted any

- Secondarily, eighty seven percent of those who didn't give referrals did so because their service provider was "too busy" and, because they were overloaded with work, didn't think they wanted any

- Thirty seven percent of those responding to not giving referrals, regardless of order of importance, did so simply because "they didn't like their service provider enough"

- Only four percent didn't offer referrals because they didn't think their service provider was good enough technically

- Ninety one percent of those who had admitted giving three or more referrals in the past year said they had done so because they had specifically been requested to

The Best Business Generators in the legal profession know that they have to request referrals on an ongoing basis because if they wait for referrals to come in, they may not get enough to keep growing profitably.

WHY REFERRALS ARE SO POWERFUL

Let's take a look at your answers from the exercise you did immediately preceding this chapter. In that exercise we asked you to delineate how you would choose a divorce attorney, had you needed one.

Following is the approach that the absolute great majority of all people employ when hiring a service provider. It has been proven time and again in similar, live exercises and interviews with fellow professionals, other service providers, and "civilians."

Please be open-minded about this process; in this profession we have a tough time believing that people actually use this approach in selecting a service provider. Perhaps, you wouldn't. Our experience, however, in conducting hundreds of these kinds of interviews with your peers is that if we had the opportunity to interview you personally, it most likely would play out in the following fashion

STEP #1: "WHO DO I KNOW?"

The first step in hiring a service provider is always asking oneself at some conscious level: "Gee, who do I know that's a divorce attorney (or "Who do I know who can help me")?"

If you couldn't think of someone off-hand, you will proceed naturally to the next step:

STEP #2: "WHO DO I KNOW, WHO KNOWS?"

If you can't think of someone, or only one, perhaps, you then begin to search your data banks for someone who might refer you to a divorce attorney.

STEP #3: "WHO DO I LIKE AND TRUST?"

Okay, you have the names of three local divorce attorneys who can represent you. You knew one and were referred by your partners to two others. What's the next step? Well, for many people it's to interview the attorney to see if they feel comfortable with that person and *like and trust them.*

How else could you possibly determine who to hire? By fees? Really? You want to hire the cheapest divorce attorney in town to protect your life-long assets from your soon to be ex-spouse? Not likely.

STEP #4: "WHO WANTS THE BUSINESS AND WILL APPRECIATE IT?"

The hiring process could've easily stopped at the previous step because you met someone you really liked and trusted to do their best on your behalf.

Or, you've interviewed all three attorneys, and like them all pretty much the same. Now, how do you make the decision?

Well, if you can't distinguish one from the other, and you like and trust them all fairly the same, you might indeed select that person who had the lowest fees. If you can't tell the difference, why not? Sort of like shopping for a white Ford Taurus with the same equipment, isn't it?

However, this is most likely the way it will happen, had you interviewed all three and liked them all pretty much the same, you would base your final decision on who you think *really wants the case and who will appreciate it (and therefore do the best job).*

That's the process people go through for hiring a service provider.

The problem is that when hiring another service provider, outside of one's own realm of expertise, the decision to hire has to be made on trust, amicability and knowledge of the service provider in the first place—because there is nothing to see, hear, touch and smell, as there is with a tangible item.

This somewhat illogical process not based on technical expertise, but based on someone's third party direction of another party, is why referrals are so highly valuable to every professional.

Remember this powerful marketing maxim: *Whatever you say about yourself is your opinion (and pretty darn worthless-it's your feeling!); what others say about you is fact (they're not getting paid to say it and their credibility and their relationship with the referee are on the line).*

People who are referred to you are pre-sold: This is another reason referrals are so powerful and they're the easiest and quickest way to build your practice.

You really have to fail miserably to lose the referred client. If you can't convert a referred lead to becoming your client ninety percent of the time or more:

- You're doing something terribly wrong in the sales process
- Or, you've let the referred lead get too cold because you were too busy to follow through on it and they hired someone else
- Or, their "hurt, ache, need want or desire" went away.

SOME TRUISMS ABOUT REFERRALS

Here are some steadfast principles regarding securing referrals. These are the "foundations" of effectively garnering referrals:

People like helping other people.

In fact, people often go out of their way to aid and assist others. If, on your way out of an office building, you see an elderly person with a walker trying to exit the building, it's likely that you'll run, not walk, to open the door for them.

How much money has been raised through the years from television telethons? People parting with their hard-earned cash from every walk of life to organize and donate to help others. Don't you buy Girl Scout cookies?

Okay, the last two examples are for charities. Maybe you'll think they're not relevant. How about when a friend calls and asks you to help him move a piece of furniture?

People enjoy helping other people because it makes them feel good. Utilize those feelings in helping to build your practice. Yes, you can help others feel good about themselves by asking for their assistance and allowing them to help you—it is better to give than receive!

Your success in garnering referrals will depend on how you feel when asked for one. Do you feel put out? Embarrassed? Angry? Or do you feel like most of the people we've interviewed for this course: honored, happy to help, often even eager to assist.

Why, therefore, shouldn't people help you? Introductions are simply the easiest way to build your practice NOW.

It's not unprofessional to ask for referrals; it's expected

How have your clients built their businesses?

Your clients' business has been built through repeat business. But how have they secured a great portion of that repeat business? By requesting, and receiving, referrals.

Your clients understand the power of referrals—they know that referrals are tantamount to the success of every business.

Yes, there was a time perhaps a hundred years ago when no rightful attorney would dream of actually asking for referrals. Then it was proper to wait for word to get out about the quality of your work.

Unfortunately, due to the ever-increasing competitive and expensive nature of the legal profession, you may not be able to afford that luxury anymore.

The Best Business Generators in our profession have always looked at referrals as their primary way to get good business.

Also, those who are best at securing powerful referrals know when, how and where to do so.

THE RIGHT TIME; THE RIGHT PLACE

Would you march into your boss' office at 9:30 a.m. on a Monday, knowing she had just lost the biggest case of her career and ask for a raise? What would your chances of success be if you did?

Same theory applies to requesting and receiving referrals. The time, place and circumstances have to be most in your favor to get your share of powerful referrals.

YOU DON'T WANT REFERRALS, ANYWAY!

That's right—you don't want "referrals!" What are "referrals" anyway? Do they sound like this?

Client: "You'd like a referral? Sure. Why don't you give Damon Ramone a call; maybe he could use you."

THAT'S NOT A REFERRAL—THAT'S A COLD CALL WITH A NAME HUNG ON IT!

Worse—if you make that call, how will your prospective client receiving it most likely feel?

How would you feel? Do other service providers, or salespeople, regularly make calls like that? Perhaps you've received a few in your time—how do you like it? Maybe you've taken a telephone call like this:

You: "Hello, Joe Blow speaking."

Them: "Hello, Mr. Blow. My name is Dalton Walton and I work for Pru-Nauseous Insurance! Bill Thrill said I should give you call about your insurance!

Great—how does that make you feel? You've been interrupted from what you were doing, and someone (who you thought was a friend) forced an insurance salesman on you. Chances are that you're upset with Dalton for bothering you and somewhat peeved at Bill for giving your name out without your approval.

You don't want "referrals"—you want *personal introductions.* There is a big difference in receptivity and chance for closure. We'll show you how to do it.

Let's now review our systematic approach to securing your share of "introductions" from your clients and referrals sources.

HOW TO ASK CLIENTS AND REFERRAL SOURCES FOR REFERRALS. . . SYSTEMATICALLY

The following system to garnering introductions was based on an approach used by one of our clients who is known as the "King of Referrals" in his sizable firm (which he grew from scratch). We've modified it and simplified it for you.

Many professionals fail miserably at requesting and receiving referrals because:

- *They ask the wrong people*

- *They request generically*

- *They ask in the wrong environment*

- *They ask at the wrong time*

- *They don't know how to request*

Because of these common errors in requesting referrals/introductions, many people then stop asking, thus shutting off this powerful resource.

We're going to show you who to ask, how to do it, where to do it and what to ask for:

- *Ask the right people!*

Concentrate only on clients and referral sources where you have the best relationships. Asking people with whom you don't enjoy very good personal relationships lowers your chances of success and increases your odds of offending them.

- *Be specific in your referrals*

Based on who your target clients/industries are, ask for specific referrals, not generic ones.

Saying something like: "Do you know anyone who might be looking for an estate planning attorney" is much too generic and requires the referrer to access every data file in his or her brain, which is simply too much work. This unparticular request often leads to: "Gosh, I'll have to think about it."

Instead, be specific about who and what you want to be referred to—it's much easier for your client to think of fellow business owners in the high-tech business located in her particular town, than "anybody."

- *Ask in the right places*

The greatest skill in the world may very well be the art of persuasion. People who are excellent at this skill know that the environment must be properly set to ask someone to do something important.

Would you recommend someone propose marriage over a candle lighted dinner in a quiet restaurant or over tacos at Uncle Joe's fast food joint?

The very same ideas apply to requesting referrals. Make sure the environment is correct—you want to put them in a mood to help you. That's pretty tough to do in someone's office, where the phone is ringing and the secretary is constantly coming in and interrupting.

We've discovered, and proven, that the absolutely best place to ask a client or referral source is over lunch (or dinner, or breakfast...) at a restaurant, away from the distractions of their business, where it's most likely that they will open up and relax—and where you have their attention.

- *Ask at the best time*

Ask for referrals/introductions only when you feel someone is feeling POSITIVE about you at the time.

- *Know exactly how to request*

In requesting referrals, we suggest the following system:

STEP #1: GET THEM TO LUNCH

Okay. You've called one of your closest clients and invited her for lunch. You know that she likes you and appreciates the work you do for her. You've helped her grow and control her business, but she really hasn't sent you much of any kind of new business.

Here's how you set the appointment for lunch:

You:	Anna? Hi, it's Ralph. How are you?
Her:	Fine! How are you?
You:	Great. How about lunch next week?
Her:	Okay.

Wow—that was tough. She's your client; why wouldn't she go to lunch? If she says "What's this about?" Just say that she's your client and that you'd like to take her out to lunch and discuss something with her. If she persists, merely say that you'd like to discuss it in person.

Our experience tells us that you won't get the third degree, or resistance, in asking a client, or a referral source out to lunch—if there is a good relationship.

If there's too much resistance, perhaps the relationship isn't as good as you thought it was.

Next, you're now at lunch. Move to the following step:

STEP #2: THANK THEM FOR THEIR BUSINESS

In having people do things for us, like giving us referrals, they must feel "positive" about us. Reflect upon your own experience—do you wait until your spouse/kid/friend/father/boss, etc. is in a good mood to ask them for a favor? Or are you one of those daring types who plow straight ahead, no matter how the other person is feeling?

We suggest strongly that you get people into a good mood before you ask them to do something for you.

You've already started that process by taking your client out to lunch. You may now be concerned that taking all of these clients out to lunch, etc. is going to cost a lot of money (directly off the old bottom line, right?).

Well, you might be correct—taking clients and referral sources out to lunch, dinner, breakfast, may truly cost you funds that you haven't expended in the past. But this is where you should be investing your marketing money: in those places where you're most likely to get a very positive return, instead of wasting it on marketing to strangers.

There are only one of three emotional states someone can be in at any one time: positive, negative or neutral. This entire referral requesting process is designed to move your referrer to the positive side.

When's the last time you were thanked for your business? By your CPA? By your insurance agent? By your stockbroker, perhaps? Maybe your doctor has thanked you recently! Ha! Hardly—this art of appreciation, which is so vitally important to maintaining and improving relationships, is virtually ignored in today's society.

Yes, there was a time where the clerk at the cash register actually thanked you for doing business with them. Have you noticed that's changed? Have you noticed that YOU often THANK THEM for taking YOUR money?

People love to be thanked for their patronage. Nobody does it often enough. Now's the time to thank your precious client for her business—we promise she'll like it.

> You: Anna, one reason I wanted to take you to lunch was to just thank you for your business these past six years. Often we just don't stop and take the time to say "thanks." You're an important client to us—we've enjoyed working with you and seeing how we've been able to accomplish your goals together.

> Her: Why Dudley, you've very welcome.

She's now positive—go on to the next step.

STEP #3: USE THE "PLUS/MINUS METHOD"

Because we don't want anything to get in the way of getting at least one super introduction, we're going to allow the client the opportunity to get off her mind anything that might be bothering her. After all, what's the likelihood of getting that introduction if she's not happy about something?

But couldn't that upset the whole situation?

Well, if there is something bothering her, and you give her the opportunity to express her displeasure without interrupting her and getting defensive, she will go negative for a time and then return to the positive position.

> You: I'd like to take this opportunity to discuss with you how we are doing as your attorneys. How is my associate interacting with your in-house counsel? Is there something that is bothering you about us, any complaints that we should address? I've decided to have conversations like this with my clients regularly so that there are no misunderstandings— so we can keep our relationships right.

Her: Well, now that you mention it, there are a couple of things we should be discussing. Your new person seems to be getting along well with Clark, but you really should talk to him and ask him. We don't have much interaction ourselves.

I would like to talk with you, however, about your fees. Based on what I'm hearing from other people, there appears to be quite a bit of fee competition out there these days. Your fees have increased 120% in the last six years. Why are we paying so much money? How much can you knock off of that?"

You: (You sure didn't want to open up the can of worms about fees, did you?)

Our fees have increased in total as your needs have grown. Certainly, your situation isn't the same as it was when you were first starting out six years ago. Our fees have gone up as the amount of work has gone up, which would explain part of the increase.

Also, I hope that you have seen some benefit from being our client. We helped split off your Bulgarian subsidiary into a new IPO and worked with the investment banker we arranged to take their securities to market. I really don't think anyone else could have turned that situation into a win for everyone.

Just as you have increased your prices due to increasing costs, we've had to increase our fees, as well. There are ever increasing pressures on us to maintain the best staff we can—and we spend a small fortune training our people on all of the new regulatory changes that are constantly happening in our business.

Yes, I'm sure you can find other law firms out there, many of them not with our level of expertise in any way, who charge less, just as you can find doctors or other service providers who are less expensive than others.

I really can't promise you any reduction of fees—we won't compromise the quality of our work and our timeliness of our responsiveness to our clients. That costs money. In order to maintain that level of business, we could cut fees, but then we'd have to take on far too many more clients, which would diminish our level of service to you and our other valued clients. And, our new clients come in at a higher rate than you're paying.

I hope you can see the value in having us as your law firm, even if we are more expensive. Is there anything that we're doing well?"

Her: Well of course your right, Dudley. You and your firm have been a big help in our business; it's just that we're constantly pestered by other firms to do our work for much less. I can't believe how aggressive these law firms have become.

I've always appreciated the way you've treated us—you've always been so responsive. And you look to save me headaches before the fact, rather than when it's too late, as have the other attorneys I've dealt with over the years that's why I came to you in the first place.

Good—she's back to positive. How successful do you think you'd be in receiving a referral unless you discussed what was bothering her first?

Move now on the next step.

STEP #4: BE SPECIFIC ABOUT WHAT YOU WANT AND GET THE INTRODUCTION

You: One of the reasons I wanted to get together with you, besides saying thanks, was to see if you might be able to help us with our business.

         Getting new clients for us is harder than ever, what with all the cutthroat competition that's out there, as you mentioned. And, we're set up for some additional quality business without hurting our existing clients one bit.

         The way we we've always grown our business has been through referrals from clients like you—people who are happy with us and might know others who would like the same level of service.

         Can you think of another CEO, like yourself, who could use the same kind of direction we've given you all these years in her business? Perhaps someone from your political action groups or business associations?"

Note: there are only three answers to this question—yes, no and maybe. All three are just fine.

Here's the first scenario, although, least likely based on our clients' success with this system.

Her: No.

That's just fine. She's sorted herself out as someone who can help you build your practice at least at this very time. You have, no mistake about it, planted the seed for future referrals.

Here's the next scenario:

Her: Off the top of my head, I just can't think of any.

You: Okay. Can I get back to you after you've had a chance to think about it?

Her: Sure.

And why wouldn't she think more about it? You're her valued service provider.

You: When should I get back to you?

Her: How about next Thursday. One of our groups is meeting next Wednesday and it will give me a chance to check around.

Will she?

Drop her a thank you note and an e-mail or voice mail as a reminder that you will indeed call her Thursday as you agreed. Remember, people like helping other people. You'll call her on Thursday to follow up. The third scenario is:

Her: Why, yes, come to think of it. Delores Morris is just starting out in her first position as a CEO in a business, after successfully heading up the Hydrolux division of a Fortune

500 company. She has some important backers and great contacts internally, but I am not sure she is set to navigate her way around that board of directors and she is in for surprises to what awaits her with the new FDA administration. I know she could use help like yours.

Bingo. You have the referral. Now go for the introduction.

You: Great! I'd love to talk to Delores. That's very exciting. But she doesn't know me. I'd feel very uncomfortable calling her right out of the blue. Would you introduce her to me by calling her and asking if she'd like to talk to me? Perhaps we could all have lunch or dinner?

This just makes too much sense for people to say no. Our experience is that about 80% of those people who have offered us referrals over the years have been willing to go the next step and SMART PEOPLE WHO KNOW HOW THE GAME IS PLAYED WILL ALWAYS OFFER THE INTRODUCTION even without your asking.

And that's how you should also give introductions: offer to make the contact for the person being referred in.

Getting back to our conversation:

Her: I' d be happy to.

You: Good. When should I get back to you to find out how your conversation went?

Her: Give me a call Thursday. I'll be seeing her at the group meeting on Wednesday and I'll see if she wants to talk to you.

You: Wonderful. I'll call you then.

You can decide what to do with referrals that won't be introduced to you.

You might send a letter suggesting that you get together or call based on a conversation you had with your client.

You: Hi, Delores? Anna Banana suggested we talk. We've represented her and her company for the last six years…

STEP #5: SEND A THANK YOU NOTE

Keep your client positive after the lunch by sending off a personalized thank you note immediately.

STEP #6: FOLLOW THROUGH ON THE INTRODUCTION

Come Thursday, Dudley makes sure to call Anna about Delores.

You: Anna? Hi, it's Dudley. How are you?

Her: Dud! Good to hear from you.

You: I just wanted to follow up on our conversation to see how your talk with Delores went.

Only two things can happen here: she talked to Delores or forgot to. Both are fine.

Her: Oh phooey. I forgot all about it; my cat had kittens.

That's fine—now she feels guilty at letting you down. Guilt is a powerful motivator! She'll give you even a better referral.

You: What should I do?

Her: Why don't you get back to me tomorrow? I'll give Dolores a call right now.

Or, she might have talked to Dolores, after all.

You: Anna? Hi, it's Dudley. How are you?

Her: Dud? Good to hear from you.

You: I just wanted to follow up on our conversation to see how your talk with Delores went.

Her: Good. I had a chance to talk to her and she's not interested.

That's fine, as well. You haven't been rejected, she has! And you have planted the seed in her subconscious mind of future referrals.

You: Well, thanks so much for trying.

Or, the best thing happens:

You: I just wanted to follow up on our conversation to see how your talk with Delores went.

Her: Good. She's waiting for your call!

Hot ziggity! DROP WHAT YOU ARE DOING. You've got a red-hot lead. Someone wants to talk to you. Set the appointment with Dolores immediately.

STEP #7: LET THE CLIENT KNOW WHAT HAPPENED

If you want a continuous source of introductions, always let the client know what happened to the referral you received. If you didn't get the client, explain why, and thank them again. If you did get the business, they'll be excited and feel good, too, thus leading to more referrals.

ADOPTING THE SYSTEMATIC APPROACH TO REFERRAL SOURCES

This step-by-step approach works just as well with your referral sources as it will with your clients.

STEP #1: GET THEM TO LUNCH

Same strategy applies.

STEP #2: THANK THEM FOR THEIR BUSINESS

Same psychology applies. Thank them for taking such great care of the YOUR clients over the years.

STEP #3: USE THE "PLUS/MINUS" METHOD

Same psychology applies. Find out what kind of feedback, good or bad, they have received about you and your firm.

STEP #4: BE SPECIFIC ABOUT WHAT YOU WANT AND GET THE INTRODUCTION

Same strategy applies.

STEP #5: SEND A THANK YOU NOTE

Same strategy applies.

STEP #6: FOLLOW THROUGH ON THE INTRODUCTION

Same strategy applies.

STEP #7: LET THE REFERRAL SOURCE KNOW WHAT HAPPENED

Same psychology applies.

GETTING MORE REFERRALS FROM COLLEAGUES

Amazing, but true—people outside of the profession (especially successful consultants) never understand why lawyers don't refer business to their colleagues right in the same firm often enough.

But you know it's true.

From the largest firms in the world to the smallest, partners and associates are often afraid to refer business to others in the same firm for fear of harming the relationship.

Maybe that fear is well founded. After all, who would want to knowingly refer business to someone they knew who wasn't going to do the job properly for their valued client?

Our clients have told us that this is sometimes not based upon reality; it's frequently due to the lack of comfortability with the fellow partner or manager.

Those fears can be placated in some situations by getting to know the other person better over lunch or socially.

STEP #1: GET THEM TO LUNCH

Same strategy again.

STEP #2: THANK THEM FOR SOMETHING

Same psychology applies. Thank them for something they have done for you or for the firm.

STEP #3: USE THE "PLUS/MINUS" METHOD

Same psychology applies. Find out what kind of feedback, good or bad, they have received about you and your work from clients.

STEP #4: BE SPECIFIC ABOUT WHAT YOU WANT AND GET THE INTRODUCTION

Same strategy applies.

STEP #5: SEND A THANK YOU NOTE

Same psychology applies, even in the same firm. People have emotions and like it.

STEP #6: FOLLOW THROUGH ON THE INTRODUCTION

Same strategy applies.

STEP #7: LET THE REFERRAL SOURCE KNOW WHAT HAPPENED

Same psychology applies.

WHAT IF YOU DON'T HAVE ANYBODY TO ASK?

Perhaps you are just starting out. You don't have any (or many) clients to ask for referrals, and haven't met any referral sources who are ripe for referrals.

Now what?

Ask everybody you know. Because funds are precious, consider doing it over coffee, instead of over lunch. If they don't know someone the first time you ask, ask them again—someone may have dawned on them after you planted the seed.

If you really are desperate for business right this very minute, it doesn't matter where you do it, just do it before you run out of money!

Sometimes desperation is a great motivator. It was for us. We started marketing to law firms by asking everyone we knew—and received four introductions. Two of those led to major breakthroughs that set us on the path we are on today. We parlayed those precious few introductions into more introductions, and more. We were determined not to make a single cold call.

Yes, we've used all of the tactics in this course to be highly successful in our business. None have been more important than requesting and receiving introductions.

CONCLUSION

In this chapter we've shown you why referrals are so powerful, and so important to the profitable growth of your practice. We've shown you a system that's been proven to work, time and again. It's up to you to apply it, experiment with it, and reap its rewards. A powerful marketing program always incorporates gaining leverage through others and enhances all the other ideas put forth in this course.

SUMMARY

- The Best Business Generators rely greatly on referrals from clients and allies to produce a significant portion of their new business.

- Many attorneys don't receive referrals because they haven't asked, or may have asked once a long time ago (and the client forgot).

- When hiring another service provider, outside of one's own realm of expertise, the decision to hire has to be made on trust, amicability and knowledge of the service provider in the first place. This is because there is nothing to see, hear, touch and smell, as there is with a tangible item. This is why referrals are so highly valuable.

- Whatever you say about yourself is your opinion; what *others* say about you is fact.

- People who are referred to you are pre-sold.

- If you can't convert a referred lead to becoming your client at least 90% of the time, you're doing something wrong in the sale or you've let the referred lead get too cold.

- It's not unprofessional to ask for referrals; it's expected today.

- The time, place, and circumstances have to be in your favor to get your share of powerful introductions.

- Many attorneys fail miserably at requesting and receiving referrals because:

  They ask the wrong people.

  They request generically.

  They ask in the wrong environment.

  They ask at the wrong time.

  They don't know how to request.

- In requesting referrals, we suggest the following system:

Step 1: Get them to lunch.

Step 2: Thank them.

Step 3: Use the Plus/Minus Method.

Step 4: Be specific about what you want and get the introduction.

Step 5: Send a thank you note.

Step 6: Follow through on the introduction.

Step 7: Let them know what happened.

- If you don't have any clients or referral sources to ask, *ask everybody you know.* And if they didn't know someone the first time you asked, ask them again—someone may have dawned on them after you planted the seed.

CHAPTER 9

DEVELOPING WORD-OF-MOUTH ADVERTISING THROUGH WORLD CLASS NETWORKING

INTRODUCTION AND PURPOSE

BUSINESS IS RELATIONSHIPS.

That's the bad news. Chances are they didn't teach you much or anything at all about building lifetime referral or business relationships in school.

Quite the opposite, actually. The emphasis was on becoming technically excellent in your chosen field. The message was, and still is, directly or implied: technical excellence will carry you far as a successful professional.

Today, in the twenty-first century, that message no longer applies *to the extent* that it may once have done. Perhaps there was a time when people sought out service providers simply by their reputations for being superior technicians, which took a long time to build.

Don't get us wrong—we don't want to imply that technical expertise isn't important in being successful in your chosen field; it's just not enough to build the practice you want in today's ever more competitive world.

> **The truth is that most of the truly successful law firms we've seen over the last twenty years were built by someone, or a handful of dedicated people, who went out and made lots and lots of personal contact with other professionals and set up POWERFUL referral networks that produced business.**

Most "firm builders" or "rainmakers" learned how to do this network building by trial and error, were "naturals" at it, or were fortunate enough to be mentored (very few). As they became more successful, they hired "technicians" to do the work.

Here's the good news. We're going to teach you how to do this, step-by-step, in this chapter. This *systematic* practice building activity through productive networking is not taught anywhere else that we know of.

The purpose of this chapter is to help you get into the directed action of greatly increasing your number of important contacts in the business community and elsewhere. Increased contacts mean increased future business and referrals as you carry out the productive action learned right here.

A LITTLE HISTORY

Back in the 1980s, the managing partner of a firm who had read one of our articles or heard us speak at a state bar association conference contacted us. Although he managed a very successful office with many fine and profitable clients, he was worried.

His office had grown, prior to his relocation there, mostly through the expansion of the economy in his city and the growth of a select few clients. Until he arrived, there was very little or no personal marketing being done by anyone to sustain or insure that continued growth. They had grown, as so many firms do, mainly by accident.

He had been transferred from an office in another city that he had molded into a regional powerhouse, feared by his competitors. He built that office, and previous offices he had managed, through organizing a commanding group of alliances with attorneys, bankers, insurance agents, etc. over a period of time. He was convinced, and his track record proved it, that without a solid network of people helping you grow your practice, it almost couldn't be done, unless you were lucky (due to the economy's expansion, growth of clients, etc.).

After a year and a half in his new office, this managing partner felt that he knew more of the important referral sources in town than all of his partners and associates combined!

No matter how much he preached to them, no matter how obvious it was to him, he just couldn't get his people out into the community building the kind of networks he had developed over the years.

This wasn't an unusual situation in that respect: many "rainmakers" can tell you what to do; *hardly any can tell you systematically how to do it.*

Thus, he brought us in to train his partners and associates how to methodically build their own groups of alliances, over a period of time, which would result in a permanent influx of business opportunities.

HOW WE DID IT

In order to prepare this firm's program, we were commissioned to interview as many network builders that we could find in his firm and elsewhere to determine exactly what they had done to build their referral systems. Two months later, after interviewing dozens of professionals who had successfully built referral networks, we codified and systematized what we had learned and conducted the program for his firm.

Six weeks later we returned to find out what had happened. The program had worked. The managing partner couldn't believe it.

We had trained highly technical people in the behavior of network builders, in a way they could feel comfortable with. We had them pursuing only those activities that had the most likelihood of success. And they had started to systematically build their own plentiful networks with new clients, referrals garnered and a greatly increased activity level to show for it.

Since then we have conducted this program in firms all over the world. It has always worked —*but only when the participants were willing to work it.* It doesn't happen by itself, now. . . .

IT'S YOUR TURN

Here it is for you—a systematic, methodical approach to building a lifetime referral network that produces a continuous stream of quality referrals. *This is not something you will do once and then leave it.* As with anything regarding relationships, it is a living thing and must be nourished and nurtured over the long term.

You will be building word of mouth advertising and networking effectively as the Best Business Generators in the professions do.

NETWORKING DEFINED

Most people have the wrong impression of what "networking" actually is, and therefore, don't want to have anything to do with it!

Here's what productive networking IS NOT:

- *It's not being pushy.*

- *It's not taking advantage of your clients, relatives and friends.*

- *It's not always meeting strangers and going to social events.*

Here's what PRODUCTIVE networking <u>IS</u>:

- *It is finding people who are qualified to help you build your practice*

- *It is creating mutually rewarding business and personal relationships*

- *It is a "sorting-out process."*

In order to find people who can help you, and then create relationships with them, you are going to have to sift through a lot of people. That's what the Best Business Generators in the profession did in starting and growing their own networks.

Just because you meet someone, doesn't mean you're going to develop a meaningful relationship with him or her. It's sort of like courtship in that respect.

HOW THE BEST BUSINESS GENERATORS IN OUR PROFESSION BUILD THEIR NETWORKS

We are now at the system we've devised that delineates how the "rainmakers" in the legal profession have built their productive referral networks.

Why it works:

It's based only upon "models of success"

> **No theory here; only what has been proven to produce results.**

It's an inside-out process

> **Starts with you and your immediate contacts and puts you in control.**

It improves and maximizes the strength of your current contact base

> **It leverages off your existing base**

> Where does it make sense to start this process of building business relationships? With total strangers? Or by utilizing the existing assets you already have? Sadly, most professionals in our business ignore their already existing advantages (whom they know; how those people can help them), and pursue relationships with total strangers first.

> **We believe you should work "smart" rather than "hard."**

Lastly, it will focus your efforts outside your existing client base.

Here's the step by step process that we have systematized for you based only on how those who are best at building productive referral networks have done it:

Step #1: pick your target clients

Step #2: taking inventory of your existing contacts

Step #3: prioritize, rate and analyze your existing contacts for further effort

Step #4: activate your existing contacts

Step #5: building a contact base outside your foundation of relationships

Let's review each of these steps in detail:

STEP #1: PICK YOUR TARGET CLIENTS

You already should have done that in Chapter 5 on focusing on your best marketing opportunities and defining your personal marketing strategy. Kindly take a look back at your notes to refresh your memory about your "clones" and other targets.

A Few Words about "Image"

Since this course is on marketing your practice, and emphasizes personal marketing and human contact, we wanted to invest a little time discussing your "image," that is, how you come across to others.

You are always marketing yourself, sending a message to others, whether you want to or realize it.

Your personal "image," the way you look to others, should be congruent with the types of clients you want to attract.

We're not spending a whole lot of time on this subject, because the concept of business casual seems to have taken over almost every firm. It appears people can dress pretty much anyway they please these days.

However, because we don't know who your target clients are, and they may be different than your current clients, who really should consider taking a look at your wardrobe, hair style, etc., and decide if it's appropriate to the type of client and referral source you want to attract.

If you have doubts about how to dress, need help in making wardrobe decisions, we suggest an image consultant. Often these professionals will consider more than the clothes you wear, but also how you come across in personal situations. A good investment, one we're glad we made, and has contributed to our success in attracting those clients in our target market.

STEP #2: TAKE INVENTORY OF YOUR EXISTING CONTACTS

The key to effective networking is to get the most out of the contacts you have and parlay your strengths into business. The listing you are about to conduct will give you an opportunity to take inventory of all the additional contacts (and sources of contacts) that you could tap into in order to expand your business relationships.

As a way to facilitate your inventorying process, we have categorized several different types of networking contacts. Since a large list expands your options for follow-up, brainstorming will be useful to prompt even more additions to your inventory.

As you think through the categories and come up with additional contacts, write down the names in the left-hand column (Column A) of Exhibit 9-1. We'll leave the evaluation of these contacts for later (Step #3), so you may concentrate on expanding the list right now.

Keep in mind the kinds of target clients you determined in the focusing exercise (in Chapter 7) and those who can help you make further contacts. To help you brainstorm, use the following categories of contacts

Category A - People You Know within Your Clients

The best place to start is with your existing client base, the people who know you and your work qualifications. Consider these questions:

- Who are your direct contacts in your best clients?

- Who else within the client company have you reported results to, worked on a project, or spent extensive meeting time with?

- Have you considered all those to whom you've sold add-on services?

Category B - Other Professionals In Your Firm

- What kinds of contacts do you have in your office who work within your industry or specialization?

- Have you considered professionals with whom you've worked in the other functions in your firm?

- What partners have you dined with, had extensive business conversations with, or done marketing with in the past year?

Category C - Professionals Outside Your Firm

- Have you included the attorneys, bankers, stockbrokers, insurance agents and other advisors to your best clients?

- What other attorneys, bankers, etc. have worked with you, either personally or in a client engagement?

- Are there any politicians or government leaders you know well?

- Have you thought about other types of professionals like financial planners, executive recruiters, and public relations executives? Many of them are "Concentrations of Power", those precious few people who know and influence many others. They are truly centers of influence who also love to help other people. All you need are a handful of these in your stable of referral sources and you will have a substantial and regular influx of new business.

- How about people you worked with at a previous firm? Might they have referral opportunities for you in non-competitive situations? Or for business they can't handle or want?

Category D - People You Know Personally or Socially

- Have you considered the people in you neighborhood who are in business or are professionals?

- What about people in business with whom you've had dinner with the past year, or had extensive business discussions?

- What people have you met more than once over the last year in a social or religious group?

- What school alumni have you been in touch with in the last few years (or should be in contact with)?

- Consider those you know from the health club, softball league or tennis lessons

Category E - People You Know from Business Associations

- What people have you had extensive business discussions with over the last year?

- How about those you've met more than once over the last year at an association or meeting?

- How about people in leadership positions, program or membership committees?

Now that we've reviewed these different categories of people, take out your address book and complete the first column of Exhibit 9-1. Feel free to expand on Exhibit 9-1—you really should have many more than 19 names to post if you go through your address book and consider ALL of your clients and referrals sources, personal and social contacts, and people you've met at business associations, etc. Look at your Christmas or Holiday Card list.

See Exhibit 9-1 on the next page.

EXHIBIT 9-1 - PERSONAL RELATIONSHIP INVENTORY

(COLUMN A) CONTACT NAME	(COLUMN B) HISTORICAL RATING	(COLUMN C) PROJECTED FUTURE RATING	(COLUMN D) WHY THEY WILL HELP
1.			
2.			
3.			
4.			
5.			
6.			
7.			
8.			
9.			
10.			
11.			
12.			
13.			
14.			
15.			
16.			
17.			
18.			

Consider everyone as a possible contact before you exclude him or her. The elimination process is designed to sort out only those who have helped you in the past and/or could help you in the future.

One of our former students, a partner at a large firm, attended a state bar association program had NEVER CONSIDERED HER COLLEGE ROOMMATE (who was the vice president of a local bank) as a potential referral contact. It wasn't her fault, nobody had ever introduced her to this process and her roommate hadn't thought of her either!

Within three months of our program she wrote to tell us that her roommate had introduced her to eleven prospective clients and she had secured six of those as clients for her firm.

STEP #3: PRIORITIZE, RATE AND ANALYZE YOUR EXISTING CONTACTS FOR FURTHER CONTACT

A long list expands options for making a productive contact base. But the most effective way to take action is to focus initially where you have the best potential for making more contacts and where you already have strong relationships.

To do this, review the contact list you've just created and evaluate them on the criteria that follow.

STEP #3A: FIRST, RATE THEM ON THE HISTORICAL DIMENSION OF YOUR RELATIONSHIP

Will these contacts help you? Rate the QUALITY OF YOUR PRESENT PERSONAL RELATIONSHIP.

In the "Historical Rating" column, rate your contacts on how effectively they have provided you clients or referrals in the past. Use a 1,2,3,4, 0 rating scale:

> *1 = Referred you to opportunities and other contacts that resulted in business*
>
> *2 = Referred you to opportunities and other contacts, but no business was developed*
>
> *3 = A strong business relationship exists which led to at least 2 hours of discussions on mutual opportunities over the past year*
>
> *4 = Not much of anything productive on your side has occurred*
>
> *0 = Other*

Rate them historically now in Column B.

STEP #3B: SECOND, RATE THESE CONTACTS ON HOW THEY CAN HELP YOU IN THE FUTURE

- What is THEIR CONTACT MAKING POTENTIAL?

- How closely does their contact base FIT YOUR TARGET CRITERIA?

- How EXTENSIVE is their contact base?

- Can they help you make contact with "Concentrations of Power" whom they know?

- Might they help you make contact with other buyers within their company? With other referral sources in their office?

- Will they help you make contact with prospective buyers/influencers outside their company?

- Could they help you make contact with good referral sources?

- Might they introduce you into the right organizations and associations that you would want to join and become visible & active in?

Using an A, B, C rating scale post to Column C:

A = High potential for access to the right opportunities

B = Very good potential for access to the right opportunities

C = Contact needs to be qualified further to verify if there is strong potential

Post your "potential" ratings to Column C now.

STEP #3C: DIAGNOSE WHY YOU THINK THEY WILL HELP YOU

People do things for their reasons, not yours. Now is the time to consider what your contacts' "aches, hurts or other emotional reasons" would be for helping you:

- What problems do they have that you can help them address?

- Are they strongly interested in growing their practice/business, too?

- What can you offer them?

- Will they help you because you are close friends?

- Might they help you because you have helped them in the past?

- Do they like you and respect you?

In Column D, list the reasons you think, at this time, why these people would or might not help you.

It's possible that at this point you may not know the answer to that question and will have to find out.

Post your answers now to Column D.

Note: Because they can be so vital to your ability to network, indicate with an asterisk any of your contacts that you consider to be "Concentrations of Power."

CONGRATULATIONS! Stop right here—you have probably just done an exercise that fewer than 5% of your competitors have ever completed (if that many).

Now, do you have any thoughts, feelings, or observations after you have inventoried and quantified your existing contacts for how they have helped you in the past and their potential for the future?

Perhaps you will agree with this observation we've had in interviewing people who have completed the exercise: Hardly anybody has ever catalogued their contacts like this before and fewer people have sat down and figured out EXACTLY how they've been helped and the POTENTIAL FOR THE FUTURE.

Approximately 80% of those completing this exercise have told us they had been INVESTING TIME, EFFORT AND ENERGY IN THE WRONG RELATIONSHIPS!

Our next step is to utilize the information you have constructed and analyzed.

STEP #4: ACTIVATE YOUR EXISTING CONTACTS

It's time to activate your existing contacts to begin:

- Garnering referrals and introductions to clients

- Securing introductions to more contacts (looking for Concentrations of Power)

- Being referred (hand-carried) into the right organizations (at the right level) where you can most effectively "network" and personally market your practice.

In this step *you will move from analysis to action* and begin developing word of mouth advertising. You will commence personally marketing your practice in a directed and thorough way based on models of success.

You already may be doing what you consider "networking" now—that's great. We suggest you make adjustments where necessary if you see a need to improve your bottom line results from the effort you're investing.

There are three skill categories we need to review in order to ACTIVATE your existing contacts most effectively: "Technical Skills," "Personal Skills" and "Time Investment."

You will be applying these skills initially with people you already know, rather than networking with strangers. This is an inside out process; we'll get to building a contact base outside your foundation of relationships in Step #5.

Where to start? Here are some suggestions:

- Begin meeting first with people who have helped you the most in the past (1A's). Unless you are already having ongoing, regular and continuous dialog, perhaps there is more you should be doing together

- Then move on to 2A's, etc.

It's important to concentrate on the "A" projected future rated people as they are most in a position to impact your network, although you might feel more comfortable with 3C's, you could be misspending valuable time and energy.

It may take you more than one or two meetings to have a "4A" assist you. And, it may never happen because of lack of chemistry, lack of interest, etc. But you want to invest where the relationships are already the best and there is possibility for more and move your way down in priority order.

Here's an overview of Step #4:

STEP #4A: TECHNICAL SKILLS FOR ACTIVATION

- Preparing for contact building meetings/lunches

- Creating an agenda for these meetings

- How to ask for "introductions"

- How to follow through and maintain control of the contact making relationship building process

STEP #4B: PERSONAL SKILLS FOR ACTIVATION

- Building "personal chemistry"

- Listening for and eliciting aches, hurts, needs, wants or desires and why they should help you

- Qualifying for "giving ability"

STEP #4C: TIME INVESTMENT AND ALLOCATION: TURNING NETWORKING INTO THE NATURAL THING

- Building contact making into your daily schedule

- How to make networking a habit

Now, we'll examine each part of this step in detail:

STEP #4A: TECHNICAL SKILLS FOR ACTIVATION

The Best Business Generators in our profession carry out certain activities "technically" that provide a foundation for effective personal marketing and contact making. Let's take a close look at these "technical" skills.

TECHNICAL SKILL #1: PREPARING FOR CONTACT BUILDING MEETINGS/LUNCHES

Most people approach meetings with business contacts, referral sources and others who can help them without thinking about what they want to achieve and how. And usually, little is accomplished. The Best Business Generators in our business prepare in order to succeed.

Before you embark on any contact building meeting, sit down for at least five to ten minutes and write down the answers to these questions:

- How can I help this other person be more successful and effective?

- How can we advance our mutual interest by working together?

- What is this person's likely "aches, hurts, needs, wants, desires and problems" about their business, professional practice or personally?

- Do we have mutual friends, business interests, and hobbies?

- What do I want to learn about their business?

- When's the last time we worked together on a client or project?

- Do I have a specific piece of business I should be discussing with them?

- Do I owe them referrals or vice versa?

- What commitments do I want to secure from this meeting?

- What next steps should I aim for?

By answering these questions you are now prepared to engage in a productive contact building meeting.

TECHNICAL SKILL #2: CREATING AN AGENDA FOR THESE MEETINGS

There are several types of individuals you should be meeting with:

- Other professionals to possibly exchange referrals with looking to develop the right ones into allies.

- Perhaps you've met and exchanged referrals with some of these people before over a long period of time, or it could be a first meeting.

- People who can help you by introducing you to people who can hire you, by acquainting you with new referral sources and by leading you into the right organizations.

In this last category will fall your valued clients. In Chapter 8, we reviewed a systematic approach to requesting referrals. That approach can be translated into an agenda for additional contact-making assistance from your clients. The difference is that this time you may be looking for referrals, but you also may be looking for additional referral sources, clubs and organizations you can be introduced into and any other ways you feel the client may help you build your referral network.

Agenda for Meetings with Clients:

Here's a recap of that agenda, which you can modify to your needs in Step #4:

1.   Get them to lunch.

2.   Thank them for their business

3.   Use the "Plus/Minus Method"

4.   Be specific about what you want and get the introduction

5.   Send a thank you note

6.   Follow through on the introduction

7.   Let the client know what happened

In #4 above, you may ask for the referral, or you may look for introductions to "Concentrations of Power," attorneys, bankers and the like or a personal introduction to those select organizations where your target clients may hang out.

One client who participated in this program was the partner in charge of the tax practice for his office. A brilliant, but introverted and shy person, he had climbed the ranks based on his technical greatness, but could no longer rely on that alone to move ahead, or stay where he was.

He had no referral network to speak of.

Here's why the inventory and prioritization is so important: One of his 1040 tax clients was the managing partner of the most important and successful executive recruiting firm in town. This person was truly a Concentration of Power who was politically well connected and built a huge firm.

Our client had done this man's personal return for years and had a warm relationship. He was rated 4A by our client and had never received a referral or introduction from him.

After participating in our program, our client decided to pursue just the type of conversation we've suggested with you. He followed the above agenda to the letter.

In #4 above, his request was very specific: Would his client help him build his referral network? Would he be willing to mentor him and teach him what he had learned in building his own network?

The client was flattered—Of course he would help! (People like helping other people, remember?) And many successful people love teaching and mentoring; it's a way for them to be immortal, to pass along their great thoughts and success stories. Interestingly, within his own firm, with a reputation as the consummate rainmaker, not a single partner or associate had ever asked this man to mentor them.

Since then our client has been taken under the rainmaker's wing and personally introduced to all of his important business contacts.

Agenda for Meetings with Referral Sources.

Next is an agenda for conducting meetings with referral sources about networking and contact building opportunities—it is somewhat different:

1. **Get them to lunch** for the same reasons we discussed in Chapter 8.

2. **Start your meeting with an "up-front" contract**: Ask them if they have anything they'd like to discuss at the meeting. Describe what you'd like to accomplish.

3. **Focus on the other person first.** Spend most of your time listening. Listen hard for their personal goals, motives, ambitions, problems, needs, wants and desires.

4. **Qualify them on how they can help you**: Do they see ways you can work together? What are their goals for building their practice? Who are they feeding off referrals to now? How is that relationship going? Are they delighted with the feedback they've received from their clients?

5. **Ask for their help—be specific**: What advice do they have for you? How can you go to market jointly? What specific introductions would you like?

6. **Test their reaction and seek commitment**: How do they want to proceed?

7. **Define mutual goals for the relationship**: How will they see this as a productive relationship? What objectives do you have?

8. **Agree on the commitments you make and the next steps you both will take:** When's the next time you should meet? Should you both review your address files to locate referral sources you should be introducing to each other? Exactly how do you proceed from here?

Keep in mind that "networking" is a SORTING OUT PROCESS.

There are going to be instances with referral sources where there is no place to go. In that case you have succeeded at effective networking: you have sorted someone out of your potential network of referral sources at this time to invest your effort, energy and referrals in.

There are others who can help you but don't fall into the above categories of clients or referral sources.

They could be friends, relatives, social contacts, etc. We do recommend sit-down meetings with them to discuss this particular subject, rather than doing it in passing or over the phone. This topic is an important one—you could tap into resources you didn't know you had, so make it a separate meeting from anything else.

Agenda for Meetings with Others.

This next agenda has worked for many of our students and clients in those kinds of situations:

1. Get them to lunch.

2. Find our what's going on with them.

    •   Family, friends, work, children, etc.

3. Thank them for meeting with you and tell them why you requested the luncheon.

    •   Inform them that you are building your network

    •   Ask them to think of ways that you could help each other

4. Describe exactly what you do and what you are looking for.

    •   Contacts, introductions, referrals into the right organizations, etc.

5. Find out how you might help them.

6. Test their reaction and seek commitment.

    •   Do they want to proceed? How?

7. Find out how to move forward.

TECHNICAL SKILL #3: HOW TO ASK FOR "INTRODUCTIONS"

Back in Chapter Eight, we discussed how to ask for "introductions" from clients and allies rather than mere "referrals."

Just as a quick refresher, here is our definition of an introduction: An "introduction" is an *intervention* on your behalf by the "contactor."

For example: Your cousin Bob calls his banker to find out if she would be willing to meet with you. Then, you follow through with Bob.

A "referral," according to our definition, is a name to call.

For example: Your cousin Bob says that you can give his banker a call.

If you'll remember, an introduction is a much more powerful marketing tool than a referral.

A vital key to your effective networking is to have the contactor introduce you. It will be necessary to get over your fear of asking people to make these introductions for you. One way to do that is to reflect now upon your inventory of contacts. Take a look at the column "Why they will help."

Also, in your meetings with these people, consider that you may go to your grave without knowing whether they would introduce you UNLESS YOU ASK. Do you want to do that?

Let's quickly review what a conversation about an introduction might sound like:

You: One of the reasons I wanted to get together with you, Bob, besides just seeing how you and Carol and Ted and Alice are, was to let you in on what's going on with me. It's hard to believe that Teddy is going to be attending college already!

You know, I've often admired the way you built your insurance business and the number of people you know. Until recently, I've never given much thought to building the same kind of network as you have because there always was enough business to go around for good attorneys.

I think we've seen a dramatic shift in the way business is being done; the professions, especially, have become much more competitive. Getting new clients for us is harder than ever, what with all the cutthroat competition that's out there. And, we're set up for some additional quality business without hurting our existing clients one bit.

I feel awkward asking this, but I was wondering if you'd be willing to introduce me to some or your referral sources and business contacts. I don't want to infringe on any of your relationships, but I sure would like to change the way I've been marketing my practice. Also, I know you've been heavily involved in certain clubs and organizations over the years; has it helped?

Bob: Sure, it's helped. Everyplace I've gone I've generated business. I often wondered how you did it because I never see you anywhere. I'd be happy to help.

You: Can you recommend any particular club, etc. where I should start?

Bob: I've always generated the most business from the local Pessimists Club. They're very selective about their membership—one has to be referred in."

You: Would that be possible?

Bob: Sure—you'd fit right in.

You: I really must get to know more bankers and attorneys, what do you think?

Bob: Oh, they're vital to growing your business. You'd like Sally O'Malley—she's located right near your office."

You: Great. I'd love to talk to Sally. But she doesn't know me—I'd feel terribly uncomfortable calling on her, imposing myself right out of the blue. Would you introduce her to me by calling her up-front and asking her if she'd like to meet with me?

You get the idea. You would then ask for the personal introduction to the Pessimists Club, perhaps accompanying Bob to the next meeting.

TECHNICAL SKILL #4: HOW TO FOLLOW THROUGH AND MAINTAIN CONTROL OF THE CONTACT MAKING RELATIONSHIP BUILDING PROCESS

As people in our business tend not to be risk takers by nature, this is often one area they fall down in building an effective network.

To keep the attention of your contacts, make sure to follow through immediately after meeting with them.

Plan on some form of communication at least monthly, whether it is in the form of a personal meeting, phone call, sending an article, etc. "Out of sight, out of mind" is an old and valid marketing rule. Do more than merely send them your newsletter. Invite your contacts to seminars, social events, etc. Make sure to maintain PERSONAL CONTACT with them.

Be sure to end your meetings with commitments to action. We run into so many professionals who have met with referral sources and others who could help them in the past, but had neglected to complete their meetings with decisions on how to proceed with the other person.

You always need to know, and they do as well, exactly what happens next. Will there be an introduction? Are you going back to your offices to search client databases for people to introduce to each other? Are you going to refer your attorney referral source to this banker? How? When? Don't leave things hanging in the air at the end of meetings, as tying together loose ends later on is much more time consuming and difficult.

Open ended meetings, unless of course they are unwilling to help or move forward, result in ambiguity. And because the other person doesn't know what they are supposed to do next, they forget about you and your meeting immediately. Complete meetings by placing your next contact dates on your calendars.

Set the following commitments to action at the end of meetings:

- The next time you will make contact

- When, specifically, introductions will be made

- How to proceed on joint marketing efforts

Database. You are going to need to maintain a detailed database to fully capture the value and control the assets in you personal inventory.

Yes, this is an additional time and paperwork burden; the Best Business Generators in the accounting profession make it a practice to apply their accounting skills to their networking as well. You may learn later on that you have few more important assets than this.

Here are the various types of information you need as an example for a simplified but effective networking contact record keeping system. Contact management programs such as Act or Microsoft Outlook work great for this purpose.

- Name of Contact
- Title
- Company name
- Address
- Telephone
- Fax
- E-mail
- Web site address
- Source of Contact originally
- Notes on Company
- Notes on Contact: (History, networks, personal interests)
- Record of meetings or contacts with this individual
- Introductions received from this person
- Introductions given to this Contact
- When and how you thanked this individual

Being adept technically at building your network is invaluable to effectiveness and results. We move on to the next skill: Step #4B.

STEP #4B: PERSONAL SKILLS FOR ACTIVATION

The Best Business Generators in our business know that the "human" side of the networking equation is just as vital—and often more important than—the technical side of building a network.

PERSONAL SKILL #1: BUILDING "PERSONAL CHEMISTRY"

Don't ever forget this marketing rule: *People help other people who they KNOW, LIKE, TRUST and WHO WANT THE BUSINESS.*

You can be the most technically superior person in your state—if people don't like you and feel comfortable around you and feel good about helping you, they won't. This is sad but true for many of us who have placed our chips on the technical cards we hold in our hand.

Unfortunately, holding two "technical aces" probably won't win the game of business development poker if your other three cards are deuces or treys.

So we'll invest some time in guiding you to improve your personal chemistry building skills.

Perhaps the single best way to building better chemistry, to develop more enjoyable and productive relationships, and to have people genuinely like you is to be a better listener.

We know—you already know how to listen! Perhaps so, but do you listen enough? Do you possess most of the skills to be the best listener you can be?

Listening is another skill generally not taught in schools. We have had so much success in teaching our clients and students how to be a more effective listener, that we often receive letters and phone calls about how they have applied this particular skill WITH IMMEDIATE RESULTS.

Employing "Active and Empathetic" Listening. We use the term "listening" in this context to embrace a certain connotation. "Listening" means to interact with someone in such a way that they get the feeling that you truly care about them and what they are saying is important.

People care much more about what THEY have to say than what YOU have to say. Unfortunately, they rarely find themselves in front of someone willing to listen without interruption. This need for being listened to is so vital that some people utilize the services of psychiatrists (and pay a small fortune doing so) just to have someone attend to their concerns.

Does your best friend "listen" to you? Of course; otherwise they wouldn't be your best friend!

If you can tune up your listening skills, you will sell more work, get many more introductions, have better relationships with your clients and everyone else and totally separate yourself from the competition.

From a control standpoint, listening is critical as well. Many people think that the talker controls the conversation. Not true: the talker *dominates*. The listener, or interviewer, directs the meeting. Watch "60 Minutes" some Sunday evening and you'll see what we mean.

THE ELEVEN KEYS TO ACTIVE AND EMPATHETIC LISTENING.

Here's how to become much better at the skill of "listening":

KEY #1. TAKE WRITTEN NOTES.

What does it say about someone who takes written notes during a meeting?

Doesn't it say that they are concerned, effective and organized? Won't the other person get the feeling that what they are saying is important (and that they, too, are important)?

Taking notes at a lunch meeting isn't easy—the food gets in the way, and it can feel awkward. We're not suggesting that you take volumes of notes; just make sure to write down the commitments, introductions, follow-through and other pertinent information on how you can help this person and vice versa. Written notes also provide the evidence, details and history you need to refer to over the life of a productive relationship.

Written notes also say so much about you as a professional: that you are detail oriented, thorough, that you are going to follow up—those are all positive traits for someone in our profession.

KEY #2. NEVER INTERRUPT THE OTHER PERSON.

People love to talk and talk. . . . .

Unfortunately, most people are in too much of a hurry to listen. Chances are, however, that no one else listens in the other person's life.

Never interrupt anyone in a meeting except in case of fire or nuclear attack. If the other person babbles on and strays off of the subject, you can always direct them back with a question and sneak it in when they take a breath.

How do you feel when you're interrupted?

Rainmakers often receive more introductions and sell more business than their competitors by simply listening more, and interrupting less, than the competition.

KEY #3. GIVE VERBAL AND VISUAL SIGNALS.

Too basic, you say? We've been to dozens of meetings observing attorneys where they sit blank-faced.

You must let the contact know that they are being listened to, or they will stop talking.

Nod your head, say things like "I see" or "Uh-huh" to let the other person know you are in tune with their spoken thoughts.

KEY #4. PRETEND WHATEVER THE CONTACT IS SAYING IS IMPORTANT.

Sometimes you have to *pretend* what other people are saying is important because you may have heard similar stories or the same concerns expressed before.

However, these are special issues to the contact and they will be disappointed Unless you hear them out.

KEY #5. DON'T THINK!

Write down thoughts and questions that come to you. If you spend time thinking, you are not listening, and the other person knows it.

It is inevitable that thoughts and more questions come to you while listening. Great! That will be a good way to keep your the conversation going. Merely note these thoughts and questions on the paper where you are taking notes.

KEY #6. DEAL WITH IMPRECISE WORDS.

Some referral sources make statements such as they "usually refer" Mary Contrary as their attorney to clients or that they are "fairly pleased" with her work or that they are "considering" other resources—What do these words and statements mean?

In order to be a better listener (and a better business generator) find out immediately. Don't let inexact words or statements pass you by or you won't find out what the contact's true motives are or diagnose the situation correctly.

Don't be a mind reader! Say something like: "When you said that you were fairly pleased with how Mary takes care of your clients, what does that mean?" Or, "When you said that you "usually" refer her in, does that mean that you would refer others in as well?" Or, "Can you expand or give me an example of a client not getting the kind of service they wanted?"

"When you said 'considering' does that mean you're ready to try someone new who will take better care of your clients?"

Afraid to pursue vague statements or words? The contact often doesn't realize what he or she has said. And, we were all trained from childhood to redefine our assertions by our teachers in class.

In twenty years of asking people to expand upon what they have said, no one has ever refused to do so with us. If they ever did, it would be a good test of the lack of personal chemistry.

KEY #7. BE CURIOUS.

Remember the time before you started kindergarten? Well, how about before your children started school?

Pre-school age children are so curious about everything. "Oh daddy, look at the truck!"

As we get older we tend to stop noticing things.

However, contacts, clients, referrals sources, just about everybody, loves it when they find someone who has a genuine curiosity about them and their jobs, interests and lives. Too few others show much of an interest.

Be like that little child when you meet with the contact—let your curiosity take over. People will be much more apt to like you, be open and honest with you, and comfortable.

KEY #8. LEAVE YOUR BROCHURES IN THE OFFICE.

Some people expect the brochure to do the personal marketing and contact making for them.

Brochures provide an excellent *accompaniment* to a personal thank you note sent immediately after the meeting, which provides one more exposure for you. They provide a written description of your services and information about your firm that people might want to refer to.

But people don't refer legal services from brochures. People refer people. Don't detract in any way from your meetings.

KEY #9. HOLD YOURSELF BACK.

Many professionals think they are supposed to be a fountain of ideas and business solutions. We are reputed to be business experts and often feel the need to come up with answers to everything on the spot. Many offer solutions immediately when they hear concerns by referral sources as to how their clients have been treated or whom they've worked with in the past.

This is not how many of the best business generators in the profession create personal chemistry.

There is a time and place to offer solutions. It is not when you hear a "hot button;" it is later in the meeting after all of their needs, wants and desires are on the table. If you start answering concerns as you hear them, you will be doing far too much talking and interrupting the good flow that the contact is feeling.

Ever have conversations like this?

The referral source: "My clients aren't receiving their articles of incorporation on time from the guy we're referring in now and they're calling us to complain about it."

The attorney: "No problem! We'll get you the filings when you want them!"

The referral source: "That's what our last attorney said."

Remember, what you say about yourself is your opinion and carries little weight. Wait until the appropriate time in the meeting to determine how and what concerns you will answer. MANY PEOPLE DON'T CARE ABOUT WHAT YOU HAVE TO SAY MUCH AT ALL—IT'S THE LISTENING THAT BUILDS YOUR CHEMISTRY AND CREDIBILITY.

KEY #10. BE YOURSELF

Some professionals adopt another persona when they meet in business settings. They start acting like they think they're "supposed to."

Let the contact meet the real you. Be open and vulnerable; be yourself. If they refer you and never meet the real "you" until afterwards, and don't like "you," they'll refer someone else in next time anyway.

It's only by being open yourself, can you build true personal chemistry and friendship.

KEY #11. DON'T ANSWER UNASKED QUESTIONS.

People don't buy firms, they buy individuals.

Don't answer a lot of unasked questions about your firm. We've seen so many professionals who don't know how to sell go into long dissertations about when their firm was founded, how many professionals they have, blah, blah, blah.

Contacts could care less. They care about getting their needs met. If you have to say something about your firm and your experience, make it short and sweet.

By keeping in mind an 80/20 ratio of listening to talking, you will stand out from your competition and develop much stronger, more personal, relationships with people who can help you reach your business development goals.

PERSONAL SKILL #2: LISTENING FOR AND ELICITING ACHES, HURTS, NEEDS, WANTS OR DESIRES AND WHY THEY SHOULD HELP YOU

People could be the greatest contacts, referral sources and introducers in the world, but unless there is a reason for helping you, they won't.

And if they won't help, you can't waste your time investing in the wrong relationship—you need to sort those out.

So, an important part of the network building process is finding those people who will help you because they have a reason to.

"Aches, hurts, needs, wants or desires" are all solid reasons for motivating people to work with you to build your practice. You need the skills to find these out, or you'll be wasting your time when you meet with contacts.

Here's how to find these reasons out:

1.   *Ask informational questions:*

By asking "who, what, where, when, how and why" type questions, people will tell you many things you might not think possible.

People, in the right environmental setting, away from the distractions of work and the office, will talk and talk until you cut them off.

2.   *Listen and feel for emotions*

There's a real difference between having contacts relay "information" vs. "wants, needs, desires, problems, etc."

It is for these emotional reasons that people will help you.

"We refer business to three law firms" is factual and doesn't tell you much of anything.

But "We're catching a lot of flack because these firms are ignoring our clients' needs and they're badgering us about it," is emotional, and you definitely have somewhere to go with this person.

3.   *Eliciting their goals*

Finding out what a referral source wants to have happen with her practice is vital to finding out if she is going to be willing to help you (and vice versa).

If her goals are to build a more profitable practice, ensure her clients are extremely well taken care of, wanting to build a closer relationship with other selected professionals, you may have real possibility in this relationship.

If her goals are to pull back, slow down, not rock the boat, not change anything, you may not have any place to go.

Be aware of emotional reasons for having someone help you in all of your conversations.

PERSONAL SKILL #3: QUALIFYING FOR "GIVING ABILITY"

You need to figure out in your conversations specifically how people can help you (and you help them).

Do you want to invest a lot of time with a banker, for instance, who only handles companies with sales over $100 million? Perhaps if that's your target market or if they have referral sources you can be introduced to.

Determine someone's giving ability in deciding who you want to be in your referral network.

STEP #4C: TIME INVESTMENT AND ALLOCATION: TURNING NETWORKING INTO THE NATURAL THING

TIME INVESTMENT #1: BUILDING CONTACT MAKING INTO YOUR DAILY SCHEDULE.

The following points will help you build contacts on a daily basis.

- Reach out to new people in committee meetings, client meetings, anyplace.

- Talk to individuals at group presentations.

- Ask clients and referral sources to include people you would like to meet in your meetings

- Get to know new people during engagements

- Leave your business card with tips, insert it with your paid bills

One of our students took this idea and really ran with it. He started leaving his business card with every tip he gave. Many of the same people received his card over and over again. He sent his card with bills that he paid. HE BUILT THIS FORM OF NETWORKING INTO HIS DAILY ACTIVITIES.

There is a real problem in marketing professional services successfully: people need to know who you are, what you do and whether you want the business in order to give it to you!

By passing out his card thusly, he was accomplishing all three. And, as in advertising, one needs to keep broadcasting repeatedly, as people forget. Consider this example if it applies to you: How many years of having the ABA send you letters about liability insurance did it take for you to finally buy it? How often does Peter Norton hit you with direct mail before you bought Norton Utilities?

In the first year of including his card with everything, he picked up twenty-six new clients, some of those good-sized business accounts.

A client of ours taught us this one—He takes an additional fifteen minutes at lunch, every day—habitually—and passes out his business card in a concentric circle to where he is. He'll stop in a store and ask for the owner and hand her his card: "If ever I can help . . . ." Sure he sees the same people over and over again—he also catches them at different times of the buying cycle.

Marketing is a PERSONAL contact sport, and he knows it! Within two years of starting this practice he had grown from being a sole practitioner to having six people working for him, just to handle the work.

- Draw up a list of people you'd like to know and proactively ask your clients, referral sources, etc. to be introduced to them. Carry this "Hit List: with you in your calendar. In time you will find someone who knows one of your targets and will introduce you accordingly.

TIME INVESTMENT #2: HOW TO MAKE NETWORKING A HABIT
Make networking a HABIT so you don't have to decide continually if you're going to do it.

- Schedule contacts proactively, days and weeks in advance, so when you look at your calendar, you already have a commitment for making contact.

- Set minimum daily/weekly requirements of one a day or three a week

- Use breakfasts and lunches, those times of day you will usually not be working anyway

- Start with people you find interesting and want to meet with the most—it'll make the process that much easier to start with

- Set goals to give certain things up. Replace unproductive activities with ones that will help you build your network.

One of our clients had been involved with the local bar association for years, serving on many committees and making a name for himself as an expert on estate taxes.

He had been networking with other attorneys, who unfortunately didn't refer a stick of business to him in the twelve years of his activity. All of those plaudits and displays of his knowledge and brilliance had not resulted in a dime's worth of new work because the other attorneys would rather do the work themselves or feed it off to an attorney referral source.

So, he gave up eighty percent of his involvement with the society, and invested that same amount of time being introduced to other networks, referral sources and people who could hire or refer him.

Net result was an expansion of his business by eighteen percent in his first year by redirecting his activities appropriately.

We're not saying you should give up your professional bar work! Just make sure it is in alignment with what you want to accomplish, practice development-wise.

- Keep score. Set goals for the number of new people you will meet this month, contact meetings with existing and prospective referral sources, new organizations to check out. Reward yourself when you reach these goals.

STEP #5: BUILDING A CONTACT BASE OUTSIDE YOUR FOUNDATION OF RELATIONSHIPS

This step is different from the first four steps, as you'll be concentrating outside your circle of existing relationships that you will parlay into more relationships. In this step you will meet with "strangers." We will discuss:

- Targeting the right organizations

- Strategies for working those organizations

- More ideas for networking success

STEP #5A: HOW TO TARGET THE RIGHT ORGANIZATIONS

Apply the following FIVE TESTS before you join an organization or decide if you are going to continue with the ones you're already in:

TEST #1: Are important prospects and referral sources active in the organization?

TEST #2: Are your current contacts active in it?

TEST #3: Do your interests match the organization?

TEST #4: Are there opportunities to showcase your abilities?

TEST #5: Is it NOT OVERRUN BY YOUR COMPETITORS?

Here are some specific ways to target the right organizations:

- Ask clients which organizations they like, and why. Request introductions to the Executive Director.

- Ask referral sources what they recommend. Request introductions into the group.

- Screen publications to see which organizations are covered and most active.

STEP #5B: STRATEGIES FOR WORKING THOSE ORGANIZATIONS

Your personal reputation in your community or niche will be built by those people you interact with in civic, business or social organizations and situations.

Since the most important form of marketing is personal, it is how you "perform" in front of and interact with other people that determine their impression of you as to your abilities as a professional. Remember, they probably have no other point of reference.

In order to maximize your effectiveness in working organizations, follow these tactics:

Go to the gold

> Be involved with those organizations where your best contacts and potential clients and referral sources are.

> Use existing contacts to help you make more introductions at events and gatherings.

Don't join everything

> Be HEAVILY involved in only one or two organizations that best match your interests and goals.

> Many professionals shy away from the proper level of involvement, or involvement at all in organizations, because they think they have to try to be involved in everything. Not so. By limiting yourself to one or two of the best organizations, clubs, etc. for your purposes, you are freed up to enjoy the organizations more and perform much better personal marketing.

Maximize your visibility

> Try not to be trapped in hidden, traditional attorney roles unless they offer great visibility and connection to those people and situations that will best demonstrate your talents.

> Most of the time, however, traditional roles in organizations are quite passive by nature. You can get stuck doing accounting or bookkeeping work that no one really appreciates because you take care of it and they don't know what's involved.

> Instead, consider moving into high visibility committees such as the program committee, membership, and fund raising. Each offers you contact with many people and an opportunity to perform where it will be noticed.

> Look to become the president of the organization as that offers prominence and high visibility for your skills as a contributor and leader.

> Seek opportunities to fill gaps and go for those jobs that others don't want—and do your best to solve the problems no one's been able to in the past. Find out from the executive director how you can best serve her and the organization. It makes sense to be frank in a situation where you are going to undertake a situation that requires a lot of work. Executive directors understand that professionals do organizational work out of their sense of obligation to the community, but also to promote themselves. Set up-front contracts, therefore, when undertaking challenging assignments for her publicity regarding your work.

Undertake only those projects you can complete successfully and impressively

Perhaps this is obvious to you, but we have seen where many professionals don't give the same commitment to their organizational work as they do their client work. We've observed and heard of situations where some projects are late, they don't keep to their commitments, and their work is sloppy or even incorrect.

You must treat your organizational work as you would that of your best clients or prospective clients.

Although you're not getting paid in dollars, you will be paid in referrals and new clients if you absolutely put your best foot forward in everything you do. You are always marketing yourself. Those that know you, observe you and interact with you build your reputation.

One service provider we know undertook a survey project for one of his organizations about member satisfaction. A good idea, this project could put you in front of every important person in the organization for his or her input and feedback. That's not the way he saw it, however, nor performed it. Instead of using the precious personal contact provided by such a project, he assigned clerical people to do the project with little supervision and guidance.

When the project was complete it was distributed to the other members on cheap Xerox paper, without a cover. There were typos in it and obvious mistakes. How did he look in the eyes of those he was trying to influence?

In another city one of our clients decided to do the same thing, except she looked at it as one of her most important marketing projects of the year. She told us that treated it as if she were being paid $50,000 for the project, BECAUSE THAT WAS THE GOAL SHE SET FOR NEW BUSINESS TO COME OUT OF IT.

Smartly, she conducted the selected interviews herself by phone, and the ones that she wanted to make contact with target clients and referral sources, in person.

She did the project incrementally during a slower time of the year and produced a survey to the delight of everyone in the group. It was displayed with graphics and charts, showed trends, and was generated on her firm's finest paper and covers.

Her personal contacts, the product itself, the article it spawned in the society's publications and the positive personal publicity she generated, resulted in twelve new clients to the tune of $ 143,000 in new business and seven referrals to contacts and clients outside the organization.

Plan your contacts proactively

Before you attend meetings or events, decide ahead of time who you want to talk to or meet at the function. Have a plan of action to speak with a specific someone, to introduce yourself, make an appointment for lunch, or simply get to know better.

Set goals for your organizations

Set a time frame to which you will give your best shot to an organization. For instance, if, after two years you haven't generated a certain number of new clients, a specific number of referrals, etc., consider moving on to more fertile territory.

STEP #5C: MORE IDEAS FOR NETWORKING SUCCESS

Avoid Drinking

Remember, you're networking to market yourself—this is business! Some people don't know their tolerance; we've all met people at networking events who have "had a few too many" to be sociable and to loosen up. We assume you don't drink at work, so be sharp and don't take the chance of making the wrong impression.

Don't Meet Everybody

Strive to meet only one person at an event, and get to know that person well. You're there to establish relationships, not fill your dance card.

Carry your Appointment Book Or PDA

Be sure to have your appointment book handy to set an appointment for lunch with someone that you find can benefit mutually from your association. Afraid to set appointments? Try this: "Can we get together to discuss this further?"

Look to GIVE rather than receive

Stop looking to merely get as many business contacts as you possibly can, and start helping others with their marketing needs! You'll stand out from everyone else. Most people look at networking only as a way to help themselves—they are "takers." The best network builders are always looking to help others—they are "givers." It is this "giving" quality that attracts others to them.

"Givers" attend networking activities, committee meetings, etc. as a vehicle for them to help their referral sources and clients. They know that what they give away will come back over and over again. And, they use this "giving" excuse as a motivation to attend, because the best networkers aren't necessarily party people by nature. Many network because they see it is something they need to do in order to maintain, grow and improve their practice and their business relationships

Help your contacts be successful and they'll help you be successful.

Always FOLLOW-UP

Always send a personal follow-up to those that you interact with. Social psychologists report that written communication is one of the best ways to enhance a relationship. People like to receive personal notes, especially since so few people take the time to write them.

Timing is important—as with all forms of communication for positive reinforcement, the sooner your note is received, the greater its impact. Some of our clients keep note cards at home so they can write notes IMMEDIATELY AFTER AN EVENT, so it will arrive the next morning in the mail or at latest the following day.

Separate yourself from the competition: chances are they don't take the time or effort to write personal notes.

Ask for INTRODUCTIONS

Don't stand there wishing to meet that important person over there—ask someone (like the executive director—it's their job) to introduce you.

Take Notes

Take notes about the other person on the back of their business card.

Build your personal interests into your contact making strategy

We remember one woman who participated in our networking training at a firm in the Northwest. She was one of the shyest, most quiet people we had ever met and was a self-described loner. However, she saw that it was imperative that she somehow build a referral network in order to stay with her firm and build up job security. We suggested she come up with a list of activities that she enjoyed in order to guide her in this process.

She loved to play Bridge and played at every opportunity she could with the same three friends for the previous eight years. Had she ever considered joining a bridge club as a way of getting to meet people? Her homework was to identify bridge clubs in the downtown area of her city as well as near where she lived.

Two weeks later she called us. She had conducted a very thorough search and couldn't find a single one! We suggested that there might be others, like her, who would care to play bridge on a regular basis beyond the same old group of players in their intimate circle. Why not start a bridge club as her way of getting to know people?

She was PUMPED. This was right up her alley! She loved bridge and was tired of playing with the same old players. She took out an ad in the downtown office newspaper weekly, in her suburban newspaper, and in her university alumni newsletter. She posted signs in the office buildings in the area. Within three weeks, she had started two bridge clubs, one downtown that met at lunch once a week and one out where she lived.

Now, who do you think plays bridge? Construction workers who want to get into a few beers between six packs? People on welfare? No—bridge is a sophisticated game that attracts a certain kind of "cultured" person. All of a sudden this meekish, shy person had showed herself to be a leader and was regularly socializing with attorneys, bankers and people with money (a.k.a. prospective clients and referral sources).

Maybe it's partially for this reason that so many clients have been met, and referral relationships nourished, on the proverbial golf links or hunting/fishing lodges. Contacts made by people enjoying what they do meeting others also having a good time (and possibly, because they were having a good time, more receptive to meeting and spending time with new people who shared the same interest).

We're terrible golfers. In our own experience, we found that the best way to promote our businesses was through writing articles and speaking engagements, two activities we loved, enjoyed and were well received.

So, create a list of those activities that give you energy, make you enthusiastic, and will want to pursue now for business reasons as well as personal gratification.

Sit by strangers, not associates

At any event, make it your habit to sit with some people you don't know. You'd be amazed at how many opportunities to make new contact are lost because people sit with their cohorts or with the same "safe" buddies every time. If you want to have lunch or dinner with an important contact at the meeting, just make sure you are seated together at the table with the "strangers."

Search out the lonely person

Ever see people standing by themselves at organizational events? How do you think they feel? Perhaps they are too afraid to walk up to someone they don't know; maybe they're new to the group. There's a good chance they won't come back if someone doesn't initiate contact with them—and, they could be a potential client.

The next time you see someone alone, walk up to him or her, introduce yourself and welcome them. Find out about them and their business. They'll be ever so grateful that you did.

About Nametags

Most people wear nametags on the wrong lapel. People read from left to right; similarly with a nametag. Place your nametag on your RIGHT lapel. Write in bold, easy to read letters: your name, your professional designation, your firm name and your organizational title.

Look for opportunities to be UNIQUE

One student shared what she had done after she adopted our training to her particular circumstances. She was stuck in the usual, hidden role of church treasurer. She had joined this particular church years earlier for obvious spiritual reasons, but also because its members contained some of the most influential people in the community.

For the last two years she had been on the board of directors with some of these important people and had received no business or referrals. Then she decided to be unique and present the financial results, as they had never been conferred before:

Instead of the usual biannual review of the financial statements, she decided to do it up as if the church was her best client.

Her new live presentation, which she had publicized in the church news, was a big hit. Her hard copies became slides, her handouts became analyses of the church's results compared with other religious organizations in the community and elsewhere, and her financials showed trends weighed against history and anticipated results.

The comments were so positive about her presentation, that the board applauded when she was finished. Afterwards, five of the "movers and shakers" of the church asked to meet with her for lunch. Within three months of her first "unique" presentation, she had obtained three sizable new clients and eleven referrals.

Regularly check the business section of your town's newspaper

Keep an eye open for your contacts when they receive a promotion or some publicity about something they have accomplished or done in the community. Send a congratulatory note immediately—you'd be surprised how few people do.

Start your own networking group

Some professionals have found great success by starting their own select business alliances organization.

The idea is to have only one profession and business represented in the group. Meet for breakfast or lunch once a month and trade ideas on how to grow your businesses and trade referrals and introductions within members of your group.

By starting your own organization, you can be selective about who you want to include in the group, perhaps referral sources you've not had too much contact with in the past.

One client did this at a very early stage in his career. As a new partner in his late-twenties, he formed a group with an attorney, banker and insurance fellow. Four years later the group had expanded into fourteen professionals and he had generated a quarter million in new business from scratch in his career.

Maintain a Referral Ledger

Keep track of referrals received and given to individuals in a binder so you know at all times where you stand with your contacts and referral sources.

CONCLUSION

Networking effectively is one of the primary ways that the Best Business Generators have built their practices. Use your limited time effectively by following the system in this chapter to grow your business.

SUMMARY

- BUSINESS IS RELATIONSHIPS.

- Productive networking IS NOT:

- Being pushy.

- Taking advantage of your clients, relatives and friends.

- Meeting strangers and going to social events.

- PRODUCTIVE networking IS:

    - *Finding people who are qualified to help you build your practice*

    - *Creating mutually rewarding business and personal relationships*

    - *A "sorting-out process."*

- You are always marketing yourself, sending a message to others, whether you want to or realize it.

- Your personal "image," the way you look to others, should be congruent with the types of clients you want to attract.

- Utilize this step by step process to build your productive referral network:

    Step #1: Pick Your Target Clients

    Step #2: Taking Inventory of Your Existing Contacts

    Step #3: Prioritize, Rate and Analyze Your Existing Contacts For Further Effort

    Step #4: ACTIVATE Your Existing Contacts:

    Step #5: Building a Contact Base Outside Your Foundation of Relationships

CHAPTER 10

BUILDING YOUR PERSONAL REPUTATION THROUGH PUBLIC SPEAKING

INTRODUCTION

Tired of one-on-one network building? How would you like to market yourself to many prospective clients, simultaneously?

Here's the good news: Public Speaking may be the fastest way to boost your practice because it can expose you to many prospective clients at one time. It makes you look like an expert, and your existing clients perceive higher value when they see you speak.

Now the bad news: Being an accomplished public speaker is not a short-term project. It must be taken seriously and will require you to invest time, effort, energy and likely, money. But your investments will pay off, as you become an accomplished speaker, thereby obtaining the results you want.

More good news: If you're willing to "pay the price," you'll likely face little competition in this arena in the town—or local, regional or national niche—where you practice.

Most attorneys are scared to death to get in front of an audience, thereby limiting the number of your competitors.

Sure, there might be a few attorneys that do public speaking in your niche or area, (most are "too busy" to consider it), but they could be wasting their time pursuing the wrong audiences. And, it's likely they're not very good at it, as attorneys tend to be stiff and boring speakers who use technical jargon that turns people off.

Even more good news: You don't have to be a born performer to become very good at public speaking.

THE PURPOSE OF PUBLIC SPEAKING

Be clear about the only purpose of public speaking: to set appointments that lead to business.

Contrary to popular belief, public speaking is not intended to "get your name into the community," or "to get the word out." That's for people who like to waste their time and energy.

Public speaking, done correctly will lead to many new clients—and many quality referral sources.

This chapter is based on what works and has led to superior evaluations by tough audiences, and lots of new business.

We have learned from our experiences of thousands of professional speaking engagements, and those of others, to help you avoid the mistakes newcomers, and veterans, make in this excellent marketing tool. We'll take you step-by-step to cultivating the skills you need to become an in-demand public speaker. And we'll show you how to generate client leads RIGHT NOW from your programs. If you're looking for tips on how to become a stodgy, boring speaker, you're in the wrong place.

STARTING FROM SCRATCH

STEP #1: EVALUATE THE MARKET AND THE COMPETITION

Before you decide to become a public speaker, ask others if they think it's a good idea.

Marketing is a contact sport! We believe in using any excuse to get in front of a client or referral source as each "touch" keeps us fresh in their memory. Step #1 is a very good reason for contact.

People like to help other people and love to be asked for their advice—it makes them feel important and boosts their self-esteem. And, outsiders can give you an objective evaluation of a situation, as they're not emotionally involved.

Sit down with a couple of clients and referral sources before you begin this project and ask them what they think about the idea. Do they know any people in your business who are really good public speakers? Whom have they seen in the past? Where have they seen them? What topics do they think would be "hot" enough to draw people to an event? Whom do they know in organizations that you could plug into to get speaking engagements? Have they ever tried it? What were the results? Why?

This conversation is especially important if you have a relationship with the executive director of the association you are concentrating on, or other similar organization. These people are usually extremely well-connected into other organizations, and simply by discussing it with him or her, you have already started marketing your services to their contacts. This person can also help you by telling you what types of speeches have been good draws in the past and by plugging you in to their counterparts in other groups.

Even if there is an accomplished, excellent public speaker in your business, don't give up quite yet. It's possible this person has had so much exposure, that people are tired of hearing them. Also, their topics might be stale or limited.

STEP #2: INVEST IN YOURSELF

Okay, you've decided to pursue public speaking. Don't make a mistake by thinking you can simply go out there and do it, just as you wouldn't want to embarrass yourself with important prospects by going golfing without ever having picked up a club or taking a lesson. Those of you who have done that, know exactly how it feels to want to crawl under a rock or die.

Even if you've spoken publicly in the past before, are you as good as you should be or could be?

Here's an investment that will pay off dozens of times in your career, whether you are going to be a public speaker or not: take the Dale Carnegie Basic Course ("How To Win Friends and Influence People." No, we're not being paid a commission to suggest that.)

The Carnegie people will make you speak week after week in front of a good-sized group of fellow sufferers. They'll give you great feedback, and "show you the ropes" regarding what it takes to be dynamic in front of an audience.

We know, you're probably thinking about how you took a speech course in college twenty years ago—well, forget it. We're talking real world, practical experience here. Don't want to invest the time (an evening a week for fourteen or so weeks), money or effort? Stop right here; you may not be serious enough to succeed at public speaking.

We'll never forget the time one of our clients decided to try public speaking. He got an engagement, had a hot topic, and there was super public relations done by the organization.

Against our advice, he skipped one basic step: getting good at public speaking.

He didn't practice, had no training, and proceeded to make a complete fool out of himself in front of 90 important referral sources and prospective clients (and clients, too).

Not only didn't he get any interest from the audience in his services (they couldn't wait to leave), he blew future opportunities to speak because no one in their right mind would ever allow him to do it again. And he embarrassed the program chairman of the organization who was kind enough to schedule and promote him. It was very painful to watch him struggle in front of an audience, but we're sure he felt much worse that we did! Don't follow in his shoes!

If you've been speaking for years, or you've already recently taken an intensive speaking course, the next thing you should do is hire a voice coach—a pro who can help you learn enunciation, projection and body language. Such a coach will help you fill in the missing pieces and make you the best you can be. Be prepared: It might take you more than one or two sessions with a coach to get really good.

STEP #3: FIND A HOT TOPIC

How many boring, stale and similar sounding topics do you see written up in your community newspaper, chamber newsletter or organization bulletin?

Your topic and title needs to be "HOT." People have got to look at it and say: "I've got to see that!"

So how do you find such a topic? Ask clients, referral sources and everyone you know, for starters. Tell them what your plans are and elicit their input. We promise you they will come up with more fresh ideas than you would on your own.

Or, read the newspaper and everything else you can find with an eye for a theme that you can piggyback off of. What's the media talking about now?

Make your title and topic "tangible." There will have to be solid reasons for people to want to invest their precious time with you at an event. By making the topic and title "tangible," you add tremendous value in the eyes of the future attendee.

You can add "tangibility" to your topic by adding a number value to your title. For example, here's one of my earliest, and still, most popular speeches: "The Three Biggest Mistakes Attorneys Make In The Selling Situation." There has always been a great response to it.

Other possible titles include:

- "Six Ways To Improve Your Chances of Winning that Lawsuit"

- "Eight Ways To Beat The Competition in the Court System."

- "Nine Ideas To Consider in Hiring a Divorce Attorney"

- "Four Ways To Pass More On To Your Grandkids and Less To Uncle Sam."

- "The Five Biggest Mistakes People Make in Hiring an Litigator "

You get the idea. All of the above titles are ones our clients in various cities have used to secure and produce winning speaking engagements.

Ideally, your topic should be unique—something nobody else is speaking about at the moment in exactly the same terms as you will.

Select a subject that allows you to show yourself off—something that ties into your already existing expertise be it taxes, estate planning or employment law.

However, if someone brings you a topic to speak on, don't shoot it down, even if you'll have to research it at length. You might open up an entirely new market niche.

One of our clients was approached to speak on Initial Public Offerings by her women's business club. She knew nothing about the subject! But she saw an opportunity. She researched the subject no less than forty-plus hours over a two-month period of time.

She took our advice and wrote an article that was presented to the attendees at the program (and wasn't published until after her speech) that immediately established her credibility in the minds of the audience. She didn't volunteer the information that she had never done an IPO, but, then again, nobody thought to ask.

Her engagement went so well she was immediately booked into two other engagements at different organizations. (Many times people in the audience will want to talk to you afterwards as they are looking for speakers.) She parlayed her contacts who had seen her speak into getting the article published. With the publishing of the article, she was seen as an expert in the community on IPO's. Today, she is managing partner and has successfully built a rewarding market niche for herself in the firm and in the US and abroad, as well as a huge book of business.

STEP #4: WRITE AN ARTICLE

All right, you've studied and practiced to be a public speaker. You have a topic. You want to put together an outline for a speech and get booked. Not so fast!

We suggest that you write an article, first.

An article serves many important purposes to a public speaker:

- It establishes credibility

What makes you think someone is going to take a chance on letting you speak in front of their group? If you're just breaking in, you'll need a reason for them to book you.

A published article gives someone an idea of who you are, what you know, and creates solid trustworthiness in your ability to communicate to an audience. It allows, in print, a sampling of your speech. Even an unpublished article can work. Many of my first speaking engagements were booked based on a typeset article that was never published anywhere.

- It creates a basis for your speech topic

In order to write an article, in the hopes it will get published, you must spend some quality time thinking the topic out and placing your ideas on paper where they will be refined and improved.

- It's a wonderful promotional tool for speeches

Sending a cover letter with an article is a sure attention getter to organizations you would like to speak in front of.

- Pre-publicity

In publicizing your speech, an organization can use your article to promote your speech to the membership and public in its newsletter, thus increasing interest in the topic, giving you lots of free publicity, and boosting attendance at the speaking engagement.

- Follow-up mechanism

An article is a great follow up tool to send program attendees after your speech. It reinforces the value of what they saw and heard and reminds them of who you are.

- Something to send clients, referral sources and prospects

An article is a wonderful piece of PR to send to your own clients and contacts, and a great precursor or follow-up to meetings with prospective clients. It acts as a superior follow-up with people you meet at networking events.

- It's a solid basis to get more articles published

It's easier to get published once you've been published. Even an unpublished article will help.

- To show to your parents, spouse, siblings, children and friends

You can finally prove to your folks that you turned out okay after all! And, it's a good reminder to your friends who should be referring business to you, but aren't.

STEP #5: GET A PROFESSIONAL PICTURE TAKEN

It's a proven fact: speaking engagements that are promoted using the speaker's picture draw better than those that don't. People are much more likely to recognize you in the promotional materials than if your name is merely mentioned (more efficient marketing).

And, it's also proven that you are much more likely to get booked to speak if the program director or executive director sees what you look like ahead of time (you can enclose your picture when you send your article, outline and speech proposal).

Spend $100 or so and go have your picture taken by a professional photographer. Have them shoot a black and white and color 5x7 portrait. They'll take a couple of dozen shots and you'll get to select the best one. Heck, after that many practice shots, even we came out with one good picture! Then have the studio "machine print" 3x5 copies in quantities of fifty (which cost about a dollar each). It's an excellent investment, and you'll need a one anyway, to send with your future press releases.

Do NOT have your picture taken at one of those places in the mall that are designed to make you look like a movie star with the makeup and lighting. You are a professional person, not Madonna. Your picture needs to look like it belongs in the Wall Street Journal, not The Enquirer.

STEP #6: ARRANGE BOOKINGS

The best way to do this is to start from the inside out. List all possible sources of people who can book you to speak: such as executive directors or program chairmen, people you know at the chamber or other organizations, etc.

Next, list clients and referral sources who would be nice enough to introduce you into organizations to speak.

Put together a "package" including your article, an outline of the speech, your biography, picture and business card. As you accumulate them, insert evaluations and comments from previous engagements. Go to an office supply store and place this material in a presentation folder (a nice folder will cost about a dollar or two).

It's always best to make contacts for speaking engagements person-to-person or on the phone, rather than through the mail. But, you don't have to be that person arranging the engagements. In fact, it's better if you're not, as it looks less like self-promotion.

Save your time and give the information to your secretary, assistant, a junior or senior, spouse, parent, staff, anybody—and have them call for you. Merely have them introduce themselves to the program chairman, and find out if they would like to schedule you to speak. Have your representative say that she is filling out your speaking engagement schedule for this year and next. Chances are they'll ask for information, but you're prepared with your professional-looking packet.

In the beginning, take any speaking engagements you can get.

Kiwanis, Rotary, etc. are always looking for speakers, as they have to fill up their weekly luncheons.

Those are the "minor leagues" where you get your experience practicing on people for free.

As you get more proficient and better known for delivering excellent speeches, you can be more selective as to who you'll want to be in front of. And get paid to do it, as well.

STEP #7: YOU'RE BOOKED, NOW WHAT?

Congratulations. You're booked to speak at Rotary on the third of October. You'll have twenty-five minutes. Now what?

- Practice until you're comfortable and confident.

Your job is to practice, practice, and practice before your dry run. Break your outline down into 3x5 cards by subject area. Take out a tape recorder and practice your speech in private. Time it; make sure you leave space for questions and answers. You'll want to avoid the cardinal sin of running over your allotted time.

- Visualize.

Before you go to sleep at night, close your eyes and visualize yourself speaking in front of the audience for five or ten minutes. See how the audience is responding well to you, how magnetic you are, how powerful you look, and how the experience feels and what it sounds like.

- Do a dry run.

Readers, this is what families and friends are for.

You've never spoken before, or rarely, and now you'll be speaking to a group of thirty business people. It's time for a mock program. Invite family, friends, anybody you can find over to your house for pizza on a Friday or Saturday night for a dry run. Expect this practice program to be the final preparation before your engagement.

Besides family, fiends, etc., you can also use staff for a dry run, on a Friday at lunch, perhaps where you bring in sandwiches.

Conduct your dry run as if it were exactly the real thing. Tell them you want questions, input, real reactions. Your dry run will remove most of the fear of your real speaking engagement.

Afterwards, have the audience give you their honest feedback.

• Do a second dry run.

Before I (Allan) conducted my first professional, paid speaking engagement, I conducted two dry runs with different sets of people. First, with family and friends at home. Then I called in a lot of favors from more friends, relatives and business associates for the second dry run, to put as many faces as possible in a room at a hotel that I rented specifically for this purpose. The second dry run was better than the first, but if it had been the real thing, it would not have been good enough.

However, I felt so comfortable after the second practice experience, that my very first professional speaking engagement was a solid winner with great evaluations and offers to do two more—as well as appointments set that led to seven new clients.

Have your practice videotaped, if possible, so you can see yourself, where you need to improve, and where you did well.

STEP #8: RECRUITING FOR THE ENGAGEMENT

Ever play poker in Las Vegas? At the tables you'll find people called "shills." Shills are folks who work for the establishment and are filling seats at the table.

You'll need your own "shills" at your first couple of speaking engagements. No, it's not illegal!

You're going to want people planted in the audience for your first couple of engagements who absolutely adore you, find you fascinating and ask questions, just in case no one else in the audience reacts as you'd like them to.

Group psychology is a fascinating subject. We promise you, based on many years of speaking experience, that you will definitely want "fans" seeded in your audience the first couple of times out—it will insure a more positive reception, boost your confidence and help you dramatically by seeing some friendly faces out there.

If you don't have fans in the audience, and the program gets off to a sluggish start, or you don't know what to do because you're relatively new at public speaking, you could be in for a very long and painful adventure.

No, your fans shouldn't go overboard, nor announce that they are planted to make the event go better. Just have them be involved and look for everything positive in your program.

STEP #9: PREPARE MATERIALS TO HAND OUT AT THE SPEAKING ENGAGEMENT AND SEND OUT AFTERWARDS

Promotional materials for the engagement.

To maximize the impact of the speaking engagement, you'll want to put promotional materials in the hands of the audience, something of value they can take home or back to the office with your name, address, and if possible, photo, on it.

Perhaps it's a copy of your article, a firm brochure, or another article you've found on the same subject. This adds value to your engagement and is good marketing.

Always include your biography and picture so people can more likely remember you and contact you.

Bring promotional materials with (to ensure they get there) or send them ahead of time (they might be lost, but it's easier).

Take some 3x5 cards with as a vehicle to have people ask questions and to close the audience for appointments.

Promotional materials for after the engagement

Prepare your follow-up materials BEFORE you speak. Ideally, you should have that material mailed the day after the engagement in order to reach your audience's desks a day later—before they forget who you are.

Follow up material can include an article on the subject (yours or someone else's), but must include:

- Something of value

- An article, pamphlet, summary of your speech, or case study are all good follow up materials

- A personal letter. Thank them for attending the program and suggest they contact you personally to discuss their situation if they would like to, or any other legal/consulting related needs (whatever you are selling).

- Your business card

- Your firm brochure

- Optional: A bounce-back card. Make it as easy as possible to have someone contact you after a speaking engagement. This card should be pre-addressed to you and stamped. It should allow them to indicate their name, address, phone number, and when they want you to call the to set an appointment.

- Prepare a public relations piece. Compose a short public relations piece about the speaking engagement, topic, etc., now and have it ready to send to the editor of your local newspaper for after the program.

- Optional: Buy a gift for the audience. You may want to give a popular business-related book away to someone in the audience as a way to show your appreciation for coming. Buy it now, before you forget. We'll discuss later how to use it to secure hot leads.

Rent a video tape or catch a great speaker.

Ever see Tom Peters speak on PBS or video? Sure, his material is excellent, but watch how he emotes and gets his audience involved. It's no wonder he's one of the most sought after, and highly paid, speakers in America.

And his material simply doesn't carry his message; if he weren't as powerful as he is, if he was a boring speaker, most of the audience would tune him and his message out.

Do we expect you to become the next Tom Peters? Not necessarily. We would like you to step out of your normal routine and be committed to becoming a strong speaker who attracts clients and referral sources by his or her very being.

If you can't catch Peters on TV, rent a video of him or someone like Les Brown (also frequently on PBS). Go see other speakers perform, attorneys and otherwise. Note what you like and dislike. Ask someone else in a different profession or business to come with to get a more balanced opinion; remember, unless you're speaking to an association of peers, it's highly likely you view the world differently from others in different vocations.

Prepare your visual aids

People learn in different ways. Some people are more "auditory," they like to talk on the phone and are apt to listen to tapes. Others are "visual," they learn best by seeing. Some are "kinesthetic," they learn best by doing or being shown the way.

Many speakers make the fatal error of not using visual aids, or using poor ones.

We strongly recommend a PowerPoint Presentation or at the very, very minimum, overheads. Make them look as good as you possible can; it's a reflection on you and your firm. You may use a flipchart with the pages neatly printed. Some experienced speakers use flip charts and do it as they go along to customize the presentation to the audience as an added benefit.

Let them know about room set-up

The program chairman, or your liaison, will have to know your program set-up. Sometimes you don't have a choice in the seating arrangement. If it's a luncheon or dinner meeting, chances are the tables will be circular. That's okay.

However, you still must be set-up most efficiently to properly present. We recommend the following:

- A bar stool (for you to sit on during your speech)

- A PowerPoint projector or overhead projector (you may have to bring one from your office; they are expensive to rent and the group may not do so. Always ask for one and have them provide it if you can)

- A screen

- At least one table up front near the projector to put your materials on

- A WIRELESS microphone for crowds over 30 and/or large rooms

- A flip chart and pens to write on (in case you find the need for illustration of a point or to use in your presentation)

The wrong arrangement can set you up for a bad reception.

Secure a copy of your outline and take your 3x5 note cards with you.

Don't send ahead any *essential* materials if you can avoid it.

Get a copy of their promotional material

Send it to your clients, referral sources and prospective clients.

This will help ensure an interested audience.

Look your absolute best

Always remember that in marketing legal services, you have only yourself to market. People do business with other people. They refer and hire those whom they know, like and trust. The great majority of your clients, future clients and referrals sources probably aren't peers. These "civilians" don't have a clue as to how qualified you are, except by the way you look, sound, "feel" to them, and conduct yourself.

Your actions in non-business environments are understood by others as unvarying from your performance as a lawyer! They have no other way to judge you! So be powerful, enthusiastic and vital.

Make sure you look your absolute best.

Secure a timer

You really should have a timer until you're an experienced pro (even pros use them). Get one at the local electronics store (Radio Shack has a great one for about $15). The timer allows you to see in big numbers exactly how much time you have left. Without it, relying only on your watch, the program chairman may cut you off when you run over. That is not good. Or you'll spend an inordinate amount of time staring at your watch, causing your audience to be aware of the time, too. You don't want distractions like that to happen; you want them to concentrate totally on you and your message.

Take a spare biography with you

Don't take the chance that the program chairman has lost your bio. It's important to be introduced properly.

STEP #10: DOING IT

Voice exercises

On your way to the program, do some voice exercises in your car. It is imperative that you sound your best and enunciate properly. Speaking in front of an audience requires much more flexibility in your mouth, lips and vocal cords.

Here are some exercises you can practice to get better at public speaking and then do right before an engagement:

• Tongue stretching

Your tongue really helps you enunciate words much more clearly and precisely if you stretch it out.

Stick your tongue out of your mouth and rotate it around the circumference of your lips many times in each direction. You'll feel it loosen up and you'll have an easier time speaking.

• Vocal cords stretching

Starting with a very low voice, slowly work your way up the alphabet, pronouncing each letter to its fullest expression. Once you get to the top of your vocal range, come back down and you'll notice you can go a bit further. This helps in eliminating a monotone and will stop you from slurring words.

Do this several times.

Get there early, set-up and mingle

You're as ready as you'll ever be. Make sure to get to the event early and say hi to the program chairman and executive director. They'll be delighted to see you early—now they won't have to worry you're not going to show up!

You are a special guest now for them, even if you're a member of the organization. Review the room set-up now to make sure you have everything perfectly laid out. About 98% of the time the room arrangement and your set-up will have to be corrected.

Ask the program chairman to kindly have your materials placed on the tables or chairs for the attendees. It always helps to have people reading your propaganda before you speak. It assure their attention, now knowing something about the topic, otherwise they may sit there for a while trying to figure out your topic as you've started speaking. Don't worry; they'll pay attention to you during the speech, not your hand-outs.

Lay out your speaking materials (overheads, etc.) now on the table they have set-up front for you. Set up your projector and computer. This way you'll be totally be prepared to speak when the time comes. Test the microphone now. Check to see the pens with the easel are in working order.

TO HELP YOUR SPEECH BE WELL RECEIVED, ARRIVE EARLY AND INTRODUCE YOURSELF AND MINGLE WITH AND TOUCH AS MANY PEOPLE AS YOU CAN. This is a proven winner in improving their reception of you and of what you will say and in setting appointments after the program. People are much kinder to others they have already met and know.

Eliminate your fear, relax, and enjoy the meeting

If you're not ready by now, it's too late to be concerned.

Every professional speaker gets some anxiety before going on. Even Bob Hope admitted to it and he enjoyed a highly successful performing career, lasting over 70 years.

The way to deal with these normal fears (stage fright) is not to fight the fear. Trying to confront your fear by fighting it will only make it worse. Instead, accept it as being perfectly normal given the situation. You're supposed to be afraid when you take a risk, otherwise you'd be neurotic or nuts.

Accepting fear and uneasiness as normal has a magical affect—it diminishes the fear and removes its power.

Heeeere's Johnny!

The time has come. All of your preparation will now bear the fruit in direct relation to your preparation. If you feel comfortable in your abilities, everything will flow very well—they'll love you.

You have provided your biography, listen to your introduction.

Take a few deep breaths, put a great big smile on your face, and thank the program chairman for his or her introduction. Place your timer directly in front of where you can see it easily.

Never stand behind a podium. It blocks off 80% of your body and is boring to the audience. It's not all that easy to keep an audience awake, involved and interested. Don't take two strikes against you and hide out. Come out and let them meet the real you. That's what they're buying.

Get the audience involved from the beginning

Leave your joke book at home. Unless you're an accomplished comedian, this is not the time to practice for cable TV.

Introduce yourself, say hello to the audience. Sit down on the bar stool; everyone's going to have a swell time.

YOU MUST GET THE AUDIENCE INVOLVED EMOTIONALLY FROM THE VERY BEGINNING. This is not a college lecture; you're there to engage in a relationship with clients, referral sources and lots of future clients. They're buying you!

All decisions to purchase, all decisions to give you excellent evaluations, all decisions to like you are made at the emotional level. A person sitting cross-armed staring at you is very tough.

THE UNINVOLVED AUDIENCE IS IMPOSSIBLE TO SELL.

We suggest starting off your program with a question or two. Sometimes, we have participants bring filled in questionnaires to the program. You can ask them to write down a couple of questions they would like to ask. You are the leader; they will follow your direction.

Even the most difficult audiences we have ever faced have written down questions to ask at the beginning of a program—people are curious, or they wouldn't have stayed to hear you speak!

You can pass out 3x5 cards for questions and have them brought forward to read for larger groups. Here's how to do it:

"Folks, kindly take out a pen and write down one or two questions or issues you'd like me to discuss tonight about the new tax act. I want to make sure you leave with what you wanted to learn."

Not everyone will have a question or issue, but plenty will.

"O.K., what did you write down?"

Now, poll them to find out what they've written. Call on those who have raised their hands or respond to them if they've started talking to you. If no one raises his or her hand, call on someone.

"Hi. What did you write down?"

Write down some questions using your flip chart. Never turn your back to the audience—write sideways, facing the audience.

"You wanted to know more about how the new tax act will affect your estate? O.K., we'll get to that."

At the end you can make sure you have covered the issues by merely reviewing the list at the front of the room.

Starting a program with questions makes it look like you are concerned and want to do your best job. And it totally separates you from every other speaker.

It's a proven fact from evaluations: people (not necessarily you; we're speaking of the audience in general) don't care as much for speakers who already have all of the answers and don't consider the audience's input.

By this interaction with your audience, you have come to their level and begun the involvement of their emotions. This can be done with a group of six to six hundred—size makes no difference.

Although this step is strongly suggested, it is not mandatory. Without getting the audience involved in this way, you have now put the burden of reaching them emotionally totally on the content and delivery of your speech.

Speak English

We recently attended a program attended by over 150 prospective clients on regulatory issues for an industry niche group conducted by a law firm. The organization did a great job of getting people there.

Once the program started, however, the speaker left everyone cold. Standing behind a lectern, staring stone-faced into the audience, the speaker spoke a language few in the audience knew and understood: Legalese (you know it well).

NEVER USE JARGON UNLESS SPEAKING TO YOUR PEERS.

It is a sure turnoff to attendees when they don't understand the terminology you are using. Rather than potentially embarrass themselves, they will generally not ask for clarification, but merely turn you off, seeing you as another typical lawyer, and leave upset for having wasted their time listening to someone they couldn't understand.

Never assume your audience knows any technical term.

Don't forget to use your visual aids and the flip chart

They will help bring your points across and add interest to the presentation.

Play Oprah Winfrey

Be open and engaging. Ask the audience questions during your speech. If you were doing a program on future taxation expectations during the next four years, you might ask:

"How many people think that estate taxes will go away permanently? Why?"

People love to express their opinions and it causes the entire audience to think (and thus be more involved).

Tell stories

Cite interesting case studies, experiences you may have had or your clients have experienced (without divulging their identity, of course, unless you have their permission).

Whatever your expertise, you might offer a few suggestions, and then explain what the result was for one of your clients.

These "third party references" add credibility to your ideas. You might consider preparing a case study like this as a handout and guide to leave with or send afterwards to your audience.

Leave time for Q&A

Questions and answers allow you to show off best how well you know the subject matter.

Tell the audience you will stick around afterwards to answer any questions they might have.

Use 3x5 cards to make the post speaking engagement contact

Marketing is a contact sport! Parlay as much contact as you can from this one engagement. Earlier, we suggested you prepare follow-up materials before the engagement so as to get your materials into the mail ASAP.

Many organizations will give you a list of attendees (it's the least they can do considering the effort you put into your speech—and they know it). Secure it before you leave or have them fax it to you the next morning.

Another way to leave with that information is to utilize the 3x5 cars we suggested you bring with to the program.

Ask the audience if they would be interested in the additional material you can mail them on the subject matter. Distribute the 3x5 cards and tell them all they have to do is fill them out and pass them forward if so inclined.

Optional: Give away your gift

A sure-fire way to get all of the cards back is to now give away your gift of appreciation for allowing you to speak to their fine group.

People love to win things for free, even if they'll never use them.

If you've purchased a book, tell them someone will select the winner if they fill out the cards for the follow up information. Have the cards passed forward and have someone in the audience select a winner. You now will have close to 100% of the attendees' names and information.

End on time

Everyone will appreciate it.

STEP #11: AFTER THE PROGRAM

The period immediately following the program is vital to setting appointments. Stay as long as you can; if they like what they've heard and seen you must be prepared to set appointments RIGHT NOW.

Have your calendar or PDA in your hands. Some people will walk right up and say that you need to get together. Set the appointment. NOW

You may have people literally waiting in line to speak to you. If you see someone slipping away, get their card and ask if you should call them.

STEP #12: CONGRATULATE YOURSELF

You did it!

Flatter yourself on accomplishing something most people would never dream of undertaking.

Never beat yourself up after a speaking engagement. Always look first for what was positive. There are sure to be things you can do better next time out; that's true for the most experienced speakers.

STEP #13: FOLLOW UP

- Immediately send a personal note and/or flowers to the people who booked you

- Have the names inputted and get the follow up materials out NOW

- Multiply your effectiveness by mailing the PR piece NOW

- Set appointments NOW

Our experience is that you will never have hotter leads than people who have asked you to call them after a speaking engagement.

Remember, as soon as they left your program, they became re-involved in their lives. The longer you wait, the colder that lead gets.

Your follow up phone call will sound like this:

Them: "ABC Company."

You: "Bob Blob, please. Please tell him Jake Drake is calling."

Bob: "Bob speaking."

You: "Bob? Hi, it's Jake Drake, how are you?"

Bob: "Jake, good morning. Enjoyed your speech last night."

You: "Thank you so very much. I hope everyone found it rewarding."

Bob: "Oh, I think so; I did."

You: "Good. Do you have your calendar close by? You said we should get together."

Bob: "Sure, hold on."

You: "When would you like to get together for lunch? What's your availability?"

> After setting the appointment for lunch, you can ask Bob some informational questions about him and/or his company. Have Bob do some homework for your meeting; it's a lot easier to have a meaningful appointment if the prospect comes prepared and he will now made have an investment in his time. This leads to a much higher closing ratio:

You: "O.K. We're set for the twentieth at 11:45 a.m. I'll pick you up at your place. Please do me a favor—take a couple of minutes and write down two or three issues we need to discuss and I'll do the same on my end. Is that O.K.?"

> This will make sense to Bob and shows how thorough and prepared you are.

> It will NOT make it look like you are "pushy." It will look like you are organized, effective and detail-oriented, all good traits for any practicing professional.

Call your friends, clients and referral sources who attended

Get their feedback, positive and negative.

Multiply the marketing impact of the presentation.

Some of your clients may now want to set an appointment to talk to you about your subject matter to do additional work. Referral sources and allies may now want to introduce you to their clients about your subject matter.

SUMMARY

- Be clear about the only purpose of public speaking: to set appointments that lead to business.

- Follow our step-by-step approach to successful speaking and you'll reap the rewards of an accomplished and sought after public speaker.

CHAPTER 11

BUILDING YOUR REPUTATION BY WRITING ARTICLES AND GETTING PUBLISHED

OF SPECIAL NOTICE: SPECIAL THANKS TO OUR STELLA ASHEN FOR HER INPUT AND GUIDANCE ON THIS CHAPTER. SHE HAS HELPED US PUBLISH DOZENS OF ARTICLES OVER THE YEARS.

INTRODUCTION

Having an article published, like giving a speech or seminar, can be a very important step to building your career.

Both of these public relations tools will give you excellent exposure (by putting you in front of the people you want to reach) and credibility (hey, you're obviously an expert in your field—after all, you taught the class, conducted the seminar, gave the speech and/or wrote the article).

Such exposure is invaluable to increasing your business and can't be bought.

It's much easier for potential clients to buy your services when they regard you as an authority in your field (it removes their fear of doing business with you). In addition to attracting new clients and allies, you can reinforce your expertise and increase your value to existing clients and referral sources through these proactive public relations efforts.

A SYSTEMATIC APPROACH TO GETTING PUBLISHED

STEP #1: THINK ABOUT AND DECIDE UPON THE FOLLOWING:

- Who do you want to reach? Who's your target audience?

- Who are the people you want to have credibility with?

- Who are the people you want to be familiar with your talents?

STEP #2: CONSIDER THE VEHICLE YOU WANT TO BE IN:

What types of periodicals might your targeted individuals read? (e.g.: business newspapers and magazines, newsletters related to their profession and interests, association publications, etc.)

Poll some of your targets—you don't want to waste time getting published in the wrong publication. The best way to find out where you want to be published is to ask clients like the ones you want to attract and referral sources that feed into that business. There may be some you haven't heard of.

STEP #3: GO TO THE INTERNET

RESEARCH all of the possible newspapers, magazines and newsletters that apply to your target group

There are several excellent, comprehensive reference sources for this information, including the Oxbridge Directory of Newsletters and Business Publications, Rates and Data. These sources will provide information on numerous periodicals you may want to target. One of our favorites is http://www.cornerbarpr.com. They are inexpensive and keep the list fresh. Gebbies is another great resource.

When choosing your targeted publications, you'll want to pay close attention to items such as who the readers are, circulation numbers, and so on. Note: circulation numbers are only relevant to a point.

Although everyone might like to be featured in a prominent, general business publication such as the Wall Street Journal, it's MUCH more likely that you'll (first) be published in smaller periodicals, especially ones targeted to your specific area of expertise. This is not necessarily bad, because in this manner, you reach the exact audience you want to target (as opposed to business people in general). The numbers may be smaller, but your article is more likely to be read and acted upon by the people you want to reach.

This research will come in very handy if you want to issue press releases in the future

STEP #4: SELECT THE PERIODICALS

Using the reference books, create a list of the periodicals you're interested in.

Note the important data mentioned above, particularly all of the information about the editor (including name, address, and phone).

STEP #5: DECIDE WHAT YOU WANT TO PUBLISH

At this point, you need to give serious consideration to WHAT it is you'd like published

Perhaps you've already written a brilliant article that you feel would be perfect for trade publications. Maybe you just have an excellent idea for an article; or, merely the desire to write and be published.

All of these are fine, because each periodical works differently; you'll simply need to apply yourself to the process of getting published, and find the system that works best for you and the editor(s) involved.

STEP #6: DO YOUR PRE-CONTACT HOMEWORK

Create a quick introduction of yourself

Tell the editor about your background—why you're an expert in the field.

Put together your mini-presentation.

Devise a catchy title for the article, describe the content of your piece, why you feel the readers will be interested in the article and topic, and the benefit to the reader from the information contributed.

Create a couple of alternative topics, titles and outlines just in case the editors you speak with aren't interested in your primary article.

Why get shut out after you've made it this far?

STEP #7: MAKE CONTACT

Your next undertaking will be to systematically contact each and every editor of your targeted publications to find out how you can best work together

You might send a letter initially, but—as mentioned in previous chapters—the best type of marketing is person-to-person contact. It's better to call first, and then send information. The one-on-one phone call will help you tailor your materials to the individual you're trying to create a relationship with.

This is the kind of phone call your marketing professional can do for you, if you have one. It is NOT a job for a clerical assistant or paralegal, unless they are extremely well prepared, highly personable and lucid.

If you have an article you'd like published, you can offer your article to see if the editor is interested in publishing it. That's why you prepared a mini-presentation in the previous step. In this situation, the best route is to describe the content of the piece, why you feel the editor's readers may be interested in it and the benefit from the knowledge imparted.

After you've greeted the editor, this initial conversation can go several different ways:

The editor may be curious, and request that you send the piece for her to read. If not, you can still work on getting published in that periodical.

You might "strike out" with the article you've already written (or, if you don't have one to begin with), try discussing other topics, titles and ideas for articles that you feel may appeal to the readers (you're prepared from Step #6).

Here are some helpful hints: Make a determined effort to check out the periodical beforehand, so you know what the articles are like. If you can't get this particular publication, try to read others in the same vein (you should be doing this anyway, as this is your selected "field of expertise" and you need to stay current on the issues, as well as what others are doing). It's easy to do; almost every publication in the world has a web presence.

Suggest topics that you feel are appropriate, and listen intently to the editor's response. The editor may like one or more of your ideas, and suggest that you submit an article for review.

Make no mistakes; this is a sales call. You want to "sell" the editor on YOU—trying to gain her trust that you will produce an educational, intelligent and readable article that will inform and stimulate her readers as well as attract new ones.

If you "strike out again", you still have one more option: asking the editor to assign you an article.

It's possible that this editor has several issues planned ahead, and only is looking for VERY specific pieces to fill her publication. Or, there may be ego involved: the editor may want complete control over the periodical, to the point where she decides personally on each topic.

At any rate, if you've got no articles ready, and don't have any specific ideas (or, if you've "struck out" with all of these), ask the editor what pieces she is looking to fill for upcoming issues. Perhaps each issue has a theme, and you can do a piece that directly relates.

Ask what topics will be covered in the near future, and chime in when you feel you could contribute something to the topic/issue. If the editor requests that you do an article about something you know nothing about, say "YES" anyway. It's likely that you may need to do research for any article; don't let that stand in your way.

This is similar to the example we cited in the chapter on public speaking regarding the woman who didn't know anything about IPO's but accepted a speaking engagement on the topic regardless. This is YOUR chance to investigate a new area, learn something, get published, and—possibly—carve out a new (profitable!) market niche.

There is no downside to accepting this challenge, except your time investment (don't worry about the possibility of bad publicity; if the article doesn't turn out well, it won't be published).

STEP #8: WRITE/REWRITE THE ARTICLE

Okay—you've got the go-ahead from the editor; she wants an article from you!

If the piece is already written, review it and rewrite it if necessary to best fit her publication and desires. Send it immediately, along with your promotional materials (as discussed in the chapter on public speaking: your bio, a picture, your firm brochure, etc.).

If you need to write the article, make sure that you understand and plan out the article to meet the deadline you agreed to. Then, do the necessary research, write a draft, and have some peers and colleagues review it.

Incorporate their material comments and ideas, and re-do the piece. Do this until you feel comfortable that you are providing the best-written, most informative article you can generate in the time allowed.

This whole process may sound tougher than it is—after all, you are knowledgeable in your field. You simply need to organize your ideas and then express them in a way that will interest the reader (the editor will help you with this during the editing process).

Next, call the editor, refresh her memory about you and your article, and state that it's "on the way" (and send it double spaced and on diskette or fax it immediately and send the diskette).

You may want to call the editor about a week or so after you've sent your article to get feedback and to inquire as to when (if) it will be published. Timeframes vary greatly. It's possible that you could appear in next month's issue, but it's more likely that it will be four to six months or even a year before your article will be printed.

Don't forget to request a copy of the publication after you are published. And make sure to secure one in case they forget to send it to you.

In the meantime, you can offer other articles to that editor, as well as continue to pursue getting published in many other periodicals. In this manner, if you persevere, you're likely to be published in more than one place, perhaps several at the same time—THAT PRODUCES PHENOMENAL MARKET IMPACT. Won't that be impressive to your colleagues, clients, and prospects (not to mention friends, family and peers)?

In time, as you persevere in your editorial pursuits, it is quite likely that you will establish excellent relationships with certain editors. As you build a rapport with these individuals, and as they become confident about the quality of your work, they may be willing to publish you quite often. Perhaps these editors will start to call you to request articles, and they may even solicit you to write a monthly column.

Every time you give a speaking engagement or publish an article, you're opening a door that will make it that much easier to get booked and/or published the next time. People will refer others to you, and you will become an established, sought-after authority in the field.

STEP #9: THANK THE EDITOR

Every time you get published, the editor goes out on a limb for you. She is taking the chance that your piece will be very well received, or at least conjure up some controversy that will attract interest and attention to her publication.

This may sound menial to you, but so many people forget—send a thank you note, or make a personal call immediately after receiving a copy of the publication. Ask for feedback; you've worked hard and gone the extra mile on this, so it should be excellent.

STEP #10: PARLAY THIS ARTICLE FOR ALL IT'S GOT!

Get permission to reprint the article and start sending it to everyone you know: your clients, allies, people on committees, prospective clients, clients who haven't hired you in the past, clients who have fired you—this is the perfect opportunity to toot your own horn a little. Make sure to distribute it to everyone in the firm (this is called internal marketing). Put it on the bulletin board in the coffee room.

By taking the initiative, and showing that marketing efforts do come to fruition, you are paving the way for others in the firm to follow your example.

Expect to send a couple hundred copies with a cover letter or just a post-it-note saying: "FYI - Thought you'd be interested in my latest article. What do you think? Fred."

Send the article to people who can book you for speaking assignments. Use it as a follow-up to conversations with anyone you meet, especially prospective clients.

You'll have people calling you; you'll have people coming up to you at chambers and other meetings, saying they loved (or disagreed with) the article. Both responses are o.k.—you caught their attention!

If you are serious about building your practice through articles, consider writing at least one every year.

Case Study of One Article That Turned Into Over $200,000 in New Work in Less Than a Year

Brian, a participant in one of our courses, approached us at the lunch break about how we felt about getting published and how to do it.

For the next hour we coached him as we have just coached you. He was a bit reluctant to do all that was required as we suggested—after all, he was a busy attorney.

However, getting published, at least once, was a long-time desire. He also wanted to develop his niche as a business consultant in his geographic area, and nationally, in his specialty of business succession, estate and financial planning. So he gave it a shot.

Nine months later, Brian gave us a call. He had done exactly what we had recommended. His article was published four months previously and he had sent copies to just about everyone he had ever met, including some lost clients.

As we stated earlier, marketing is a contact sport. Prospective buyers are always some place in a "buying cycle" between "not interested" to "let's do it."

Brian caught four people he had met and spoken to previously at the prime time in the buying cycle who were now ready to hire him, and *three clients who had fired him over high fees who wanted to re-hire him.*

He parlayed the article into three local speaking engagements, picking up another eight clients and was scheduled to speak at a national conference in front of two hundred potential clients eight months down the road.

He contracted for two additional articles with the same publication and three articles in other publications.

Net result, in nine months from one article: over $200,000 in new business.

CONCLUSION

Getting published, like other marketing endeavors, is not always easy. It requires you to exert a certain amount of initiative and effort.

However, the key element is often the desire to see your article and your name in print. If this desire is strong enough, it will sustain you through the challenge of researching publications and contacting editors, writing articles and doing follow-up work.

Throughout this process, always remember that there are many potential rewards at stake: by publishing an article in a professional periodical, you are establishing yourself as an expert in your field. You are calling attention to yourself, in a most positive manner. Clients, potential clients, referral sources, peers, friends, and relatives will likely be quite impressed with your achievements in this area. You will command new respect and credibility.

Handled properly, a published article cannot help but increase your bottom line. The more you pursue this marketing mechanism, the more exposure you'll get, and the greater effect you'll see on the growth of your practice.

So, take these ideas and get to work!!! We'll be looking for you—in print!

SUMMARY

- Having an article published, like giving a speech or seminar, can be a very important step to building your career by giving you excellent exposure in front of the right people and credibility as an expert in your field

- It's much easier for potential clients to buy your services when they regard you as an authority in your field

- Use our systematic approach to getting published:

  Step #1: Think about and decide upon whom you want to reach

  Step #2: Consider the vehicle you want to do that with

  Step #3: Go to the internet and RESEARCH

  Step #4: Select the periodicals

  Step #5: Decide what you want to publish

  Step #6: Do your pre-contact homework

  Step #7: Make contact

Step #8: Write/Rewrite the article

Step #9: Thank the editor

Step #10: Parlay the article for all it's got

- The key element to getting published is often the desire to see your article and your name in print.

MY PERSONAL MARKETING PLAN
BY ALLAN S. BORESS, CPA, CFE

INTRODUCTION

We have now come to the conclusion of this book, so I thought I would share with you my own personal marketing plan.

This plan has led me to become the foremost consultant to the professions in the areas of business development, sales and personal marketing, and client retention strategies.

NOBODY has trained more professionals (over 200,000) since 1980 all over the world as I have. I have published over 300 articles and had eight books published. My I Hate Selling Book is the standard for selling professional services in the professions. I have worked with over 500 professional service firms, some of the largest in the world (visit my web site www.allanboress.com for a client list) including the Big Four Consulting Firms.

This is not meant to brag, but to prove an important point: our firm has followed every idea in this course and it has paid off.

GOOD MARKETING AND PERSONAL ADVICE

Every morning I spend some time with the Lord.

This habit started in 1983 and has allowed me to develop a very personal relationship with God, and a great deal of peace of mind and strength in a confusing world and challenging business.

People often ask me how one maintains a travel schedule of 100+ cities a year, sometimes five or six in one week. Travel today is a miserable, draining experience, yet one has to be full of energy when one takes the platform in front of an audience, be they sixteen in number or six hundred.

My daily quiet time gives me that energy, as it is coming from the Source of energy in the universe.

This very morning, I was spending some time with Ruth Stafford Peale. She is the widow of the beloved and famous Norman Vincent Peale, author of one of the best selling books of all time, *The Power of Positive Thinking*, which I strongly recommend. I also advise you to visit their website, www.guideposts.org and order their monthly magazine *Guideposts* as well as their new *Positive Thinking* magazine. What a way to start the day!

In this morning's quiet time, Mrs. Peale was making a reference to John Segal, president of North American Products, who communicates his step-by-step plan of success to visiting students from inner city schools.

Segal says one can avoid a life of poverty and welfare and *lead a fulfilled life* by first following three basic goals:

1. *Don't get pregnant (or impregnate someone) before high school graduation and marriage*

2. *Get married and stay married*

3. *Get a job (almost any job) and keep it*

In today's politically correct society, these common sense ideas are dismissed as being old fashioned or even absurd. But think about it—it's pretty good advice for anyone.

After understanding there are only three goals that will keep one from poverty, Segal then shares his next three "higher goals":

4. *Work hard on your job, but work harder on improving yourself (and make yourself more valuable to your employer, to clients, and to society in general)*

5. *Write down your life goals and concentrate on achieving them (Charles Ross writes in* New Man *magazine that only 3% of the population hit their goals 90% of the time and that these are the same 3% who write down their goals)*

6. *Seek a positive, powerful relationship with God*

MORE GOOD ADVICE

Mrs. Peale (who is in her nineties) writes, "Don't wait for success to find you—that's unproductive and will get you nowhere. Be open to new ideas and projects. In your church (synagogue) or community, through your school or job, you can seek out ways to learn and gain experience in various fields. *One opportunity often leads to another* (italics mine). Use each experience as a springboard or as a stepping-stone to the next. *Keep alert and aware of what's happening around you, and you will see opportunities in abundance* (italics mine).

"Also, develop a magnetic, appealing personality. Think of yourself as full of vitality and enthusiasm, ready to tackle any challenge that crosses your path. The law of magnetic attraction will draw opportunities to you as sure as bees are attracted to honey. Model yourself after those who have succeeded before you. Make them your heroes. Get to know what has worked for them and adapt their methods to your own plan of success."

Wow—sounds like Mrs. Peale read our course! What a wonderful summary of ideas.

Mrs. Peale concludes with valuable advice: "You may have a lifetime of dreams that are begging to be brought into reality, so believe that God has given them to you as a special gift. Hold on to the deep belief that He will help you."

MY PERSONAL MARKETING PLAN

Over the years many people have asked about my own personal marketing plan. I believe we can summarize it into a few steps:

1. *I Ask God to guide me*

   I ask that He put me in front of those people He wants me to help.

   Now, I never thought, nor asked, that He send these people walking by my desk in my office. Rather, I felt my part of the bargain was to be in a position where they could most readily find me. So …

2. *I write ideas down that I should do*

   To put me in the flow of prospects and referral sources to have people find me. Unlike most consultants and professionals, I keep a list with me at all times of action steps to take as it relates to marketing.

   What I have noticed is that neat marketing ideas can come at any time: in the middle of the night, driving down the street, in the shower, on a golf course, or in church.

   The difference is I don't let them pass … I capture these nuggets and never dismiss any as being foolish.

3. *Then we do some*

   We do lots and lots of high-impact marketing activities (ones that will attract a great deal of attention because of where they are conducted or placed, who they are in front of, and the content of the speech, article or seminar.

   We try for at least 10 high-impact marketing activities a year, in addition to the MULTITUDES of the regular articles, direct mail, speeches we do.

   Quantity equals quality in marketing, remember?

4. *A style to remember*

   There are at least three radio personalities one can think off the top of their head who stand above all the others in terms of popularity and success. All three of these people make many millions of dollars a year. It's hard to argue with that kind of success.

   Dr. Laura Schlesinger, Howard Stern and Rush Limbaugh are the most successful in their very competitive business. What do they have in common? *People don't forget them once they have heard them.* Whether you agree with their viewpoint or style or not, theirs is an effective marketing tool because they generate an emotional response. *The uninvolved party is impossible to sell.*

   I have a style that people will remember (dynamic, different, funny). You will never see anyone leave one of my seminars, even to use the washroom.

Recently I did a web chatroom seminar where people could only read as I typed. The comments still came back "memorable," "unique style and message … "

5.   *I understand that nobody sells everybody*

Some opportunities aren't meant to be, no matter how hard you try. Your job is to do your best to impact your market.

CONCLUSION

One of our greatest presidents, Teddy Roosevelt, wrote the following words.

> *"It's not the critic that counts, not the man who points out how the strong man stumbled or whether the doers of deeds could have actually done them better. The credit belongs to the man who is actually in the arena, whose face is marred by dust and sweat and blood, who strives valiantly, who errs, and often comes up short again and again. Who knows the great enthusiasms, the great devotions, and spends himself in a worthy cause. And who, if at best in the end, knows the triumph of higher treatment and high achievement. And who at worst, if he fails, at least fails while daring greatly so that his soul shall never be with those cold and timid ones who know neither victory nor defeat."*

Now go get in that arena!

APPENDIX: TRAINING FROM ALLAN BORESS & ASSOCIATES AND SAGE

Contact mailto:info@sagelawmarketing.com

OVERVIEW

Nobody we can find has trained more professionals in the arts of

- Selling their ideas

- Closing more deals

- Productive personal marketing

- Superior client relationship management

We have worked with both industry-leading firms and scores of mid-size and smaller firms.

We leverage the Best Practices of top producers across the professions and transfer these skills to your attorneys. We have a 20+ year track record of results.

Review the specific courses below:

1. **Building The Entrepreneurial Skills of Attorneys:** *We offer world-class in-house training and coaching programs for attorneys.*

2. **E-Training Programs:** *We offer module-based training than can be conducted as a complement to our live training—and in open sessions as well.*

3. **Best Practices Forums For Law Firm Marketing Directors:** *We offer small group training and individual coaching to develop the skills of law firm marketing directors.*

4. **Client and Market Research:** *We provide the customer and market insights to strengthen your service line marketing and sales performance.*

5. **In-House and Association-Sponsored Training**

SAGE and Allan Boress & Associate partner to provide these four categories of services to the legal community. All are practical and proven sessions taught in a highly interactive fashion. Lessons are all based on our work with top rainmakers.

BUILDING YOUR PERSONAL REPUTATION

Become a celebrity in your field. Let prospects know why they should be working with you—instead of a similarly qualified attorney.

NETWORKING

Build a wide and proactive network of fertile referral sources

PROFESSIONAL SELLING

Win more business by leveraging your existing strengths as an attorney and separate yourself from the competition.

CLIENT RELATIONSHIP MANAGEMENT

Build your most precious asset: your relationship with your clients. Establish world class working relations, sell additional services and turn your clients into your sales force.

VIRTUAL BUSINESS DEVELOPMENT TRAINING AND COACHING FOR ATTORNEYS

Until recently, we did all of our training on an in-house basis. Frankly, this approach still provides the best results for firms will to make the commitment and investment.

Since attorneys are busy and their time precious, it may be difficult for them to go off and attend multiple day seminars on business development. In addition, the impact of one-time training courses wears off quickly and attorneys can quickly fall back into bad habits. So, we recently came up with an innovative way to deliver the training in monthly "e-modules".

Here is what we offer on an open basis:

- Each month you get a training module (summary of best practices, key skills and action planning exercise) with an "e-book" that enables individual attorneys to put the ideas to work.

- We then run a 1–2 hour web-seminar to review the training. The topics we will cover for the next 6 months are:

Best Practices Forums And Coaching For Law Firm Marketing Directors

Being a marketing director is a challenging—and sometimes a lonely & frustrating profession. There are few places to turn for professional development and coaching. Starting in January, we will hold monthly best practices web forums for small groups (8–10)—usually 2 hours in length. We offer the first one free.

Client and Market Research

Successful marketing has to be grounded in customer and market realities. Service must be geared to clients "pain" and be communicated in terms that clients value. Critical wins and losses must be diagnosed. The quality of your client relationships must be audited.

We provide the following services: focus groups, client interviews, referral source interviews, and market analysis. We can support:

1. *Branding and positioning*

2. *Service line marketing*

3. *Client relationship quality programs*

4. *Win/loss analysis*

WE SHOW YOU HOW TO DESIGN AND EXECUTE WORLD CLASS MARKETING PROGRAMS THAT RESULT IN QUALITY NEW CLIENTS AND BUSINESS.

TOPIC INDEX